Encyclopedia of
CREATIVE COOKING

Volume 3
Beef & Veal

D1529714

Editors for U.S. editions
Steve Sherman and Julia Older

ECB Enterprises Inc.

Beef has always enjoyed a sumptuous reputation — it became famous as the 'roast beef of Olde England' and was even knighted by King Henry VIII, after which the two hindquarters, including the legs, rump, sirloin and wing ribs, were always referred to as *Baronne de Boeuf*.

Beef is very nutritious and a good source of energy. It is rich in protein, vitamin B and iron. The price of beef varies with the cut. The most expensive are usually the most tender and can be quickroasted, fried or broiled. Tougher cheaper cuts require slower cooking methods to tenderize them but are just as nutritious.

Beef is extremely versatile and can be prepared and cooked in so many ways. You can roast, fry, broil, casserole, pot-roast, stew, boil, braise, stuff, smoke or salt it. It can be ground and made into hamburgers, or baked *en croûte* in pastry. Of course, the method of cooking you use will depend on the cut and quality of the beef and how much you can afford to spend.

Choosing Beef
When choosing beef, always take the color and texture into account. The lean flesh should be light rosy or cherry red in color, and the fat should be a creamy yellow. The lean meat should be marbled with fat — this is always a sign of good quality, tender meat. There should be a minimum of gristle. The texture will determine the tenderness of the meat — the most tender cuts such as sirloin spring back when touched.

Cuts of Beef
Different cuts will require different methods of cooking. Always be sure that you choose the right one. Cuts vary from one country to another, and even between areas and districts. Many cuts such as rib, chuck, leg, skirt, blade, shin, top round and brisket are very similar. The main differences lie in the cutting and terminology used, especially with steaks. The American equivalent of British fillet steak is tenderloin. As well as sirloin steak,

there are T-bone, Porterhouse, pin bone, and Club or Delmonico steaks. All these steaks are now popular.

Storing Beef
Store raw meat loosely wrapped in a cool place or refrigerator. Beef will keep in a refrigerator for 2-3 days. The most economical way to buy beef is in bulk if you have a freezer. The recommended storage time in a freezer is 8 months. Always thaw out frozen meat either in the refrigerator or at room temperature slowly. Never immerse in hot water to speed up the process. Once it is thawed, you should never refreeze the beef.

Seasoning Beef
Always season beef after cooking, especially roasting or broiling, with salt and freshly ground black pepper. Salt draws out the juices. For additional flavor you can season the beef with herbs or spices. Try rubbing the roast with garlic, onion, herbs or spices before cooking, or insert a clove of garlic or a small piece of onion into the meat itself.

Improving the Texture and Flavor of Beef
One way to improve the texture and flavor of cheaper cuts of meat is to marinate them for several hours. Try using wine, beer or cider or an acidic mixture of fruit juices and vinegar. You can tenderize a tough steak or roast with a ready-made tenderizer, which most supermarkets sell. These tenderizing powders are usually prepared from extract of figs, papain (an enzyme of papaya) and pineapple — the fresh juice of these fruits works equally well.

Larding Beef
You can lard tough, cheaper cuts of meat with a larding needle to tenderize them. Just push a larding needle through the meat with the grain, thread with fat and pull back through. This is explained in the step-by-step photo guide to larding on page 222. Introducing the fat into the flesh will moisten the meat during cooking.

Steaks

The most popular and well-known steak cuts are — in usual order of costliness — tenderloin, sirloin, rib, and rump. Being very expensive, tenderloin is graded into several different cuts.

An average beef tenderloin is 18-20 inches in length and tapers in width from 4 inches to 1 inch. A whole tenderloin weighs from 6-9 lbs. untrimmed, and when prepared for cooking, a tenderloin will weigh on average 3½-4 lbs.

The Châteaubriand is taken from the head of the tenderloin. A piece 4 inches is cut off, weighing from 12-16 ozs. It is wrapped with a cloth, and flattened until it is 2 inches thick, widening to double its original size at 8 inches in diameter. When cooked it is served in slices, and is always for two.

The Coeur de Filet or Medallion steak is cut 1 inch thick, and weighs ½ lb. It is cut from the heart of the tenderloin, and is also flattened to a diameter of 3 inches. The tenderloin steak is cut from the middle of the tenderloin, 2½ inches thick, about 4 inches in diameter, and weighs 7 ozs.

Sirloin steaks are tender and flavorsome. Entrecôte means 'between the ribs' but the term now includes any sirloin steak. Porterhouse is another cut of the sirloin. Rib steaks are large and tasty. The famous T-bone steak includes part of the tenderloin and sirloin. Rump steak is often hung to mature, producing a fine flavor.

The Tournedos is also cut from the middle of the tenderloin. It is tied in a blanched slice of bacon before cooking. It is cut 1½ inches thick, 3 inches in diameter, and weighs 5 ozs. Filet Mignon is cut from the thin end in a triangular shape, and weighs $\frac{1}{4}$ lb. This end of the tenderloin is also used for Strogonoff where the steak is cut into strips $1 \times \frac{1}{4}$ inch, or raw for Steak Tartare.

The cooking times will vary with the method used and the type and thickness of steak, but in general 2 minutes of cooking (1 minute each side) produces a rare steak, 4 minutes a medium steak, and 8-12 minutes a well-done one. Broiling is suitable for the best types of steak, while cheaper cuts may be fried very quickly.

Apollo Steaks

2 tablespoons oil
4 sirloin or rump steaks

For the Sauce:
1 lamb or beef kidney, skinned, cored and sliced
2 tablespoons butter
1 large onion, sliced
2 tomatoes, skinned, seeded and chopped
1 green pepper, seeded and chopped

Juicy Apollo Steaks are dressed with a richly flavored sauce of kidneys, green pepper, tomato and onion

$\frac{2}{3}$ cup red wine
$\frac{2}{3}$ cup beef stock
salt and pepper
pinch oregano

1 Sauté the sauce ingredients, except the wine, stock and seasonings, in a saucepan for 5 minutes until they are tender. Add the wine and stock, and season with salt, pepper and a pinch of oregano. Bring to a boil and simmer for 5 minutes to thicken.

2 Heat the oil in a skillet and fry the steaks for 2-8 minutes or according to taste. Pour the sauce over them and serve immediately. Serve with buttered new potatoes and a green or mixed salad.

Serves 4

Steak au Poivre Vert

4 sirloin steaks, ½ inch thick
¼ cup oil
pinch salt
¼ cup butter
3 tablespoons brandy
½ cup dry sherry or Madeira
1 medium onion, chopped
2 tablespoons green peppercorns,
  canned
2 tablespoons soy sauce
1 teaspoon vinegar
⅔ cup light cream
pinch paprika
1 tablespoon chopped fresh
  parsley

1 Trim the steaks of any excess fat and sinew. Brush with a little oil and season very lightly with salt.

2 Heat the rest of the oil and butter in a skillet and quickly fry the steaks on both sides to sear the flesh, for about 2 minutes. Pour in the brandy and ignite it. Almost immediately, pour in the sherry or Madeira to put out the brandy flames. Remove the steaks and keep them warm while cooking the sauce.

3 To the mixture in the pan add the onion, peppercorns, soy sauce, and vinegar. Boil for 4 minutes. Add the cream and paprika and boil briskly for another minute.

4 Return the steaks to the sauce to reheat for a minute on each side. Serve immediately, garnished with the chopped parsley.

Serves 4

Steak au Poivre Vert has the real taste of luxury, with brandy to flame, wine, and mildly spicy green peppercorns

Tips: Green peppercorns are the fresh berries of the spice more commonly used in its dried form as black or white ground pepper. They are available in canned form, and have a mild and aromatic flavor.

The given cooking times for sirloin steak are designed for a rare-cooked steak of ½ inch thick. Thicker steaks should be fried for twice the given length of time, or beaten with a rolling pin or meat mallet to the given thickness. For a medium-cooked steak, fry for 4 minutes. For a well-cooked steak, cover the skillet while frying for 4 or 5 minutes.

Entrecôte Bordelaise

4 sirloin steaks, about 1½ inches
  thick
2 tablespoons oil
salt and pepper
1 tablespoon chopped fresh
  parsley

For the Bordelaise Sauce:
4 shallots or 1 onion, chopped
¾ cup dry red wine
bouquet garni
3 tablespoons meat juice
¾ cup beef stock
1 tablespoon tomato paste
1 tablespoon beef fat
2 tablespoons flour

1 Brush the steaks with the oil and broil them for 8-12 minutes according to taste, turning once. Reserve the meat juices and keep the steaks warm.

2 To make the sauce, boil the shallot or onion in the wine, with the bouquet garni, for 5 minutes. Stir in the meat juice, beef stock and tomato paste.

3 Make a roux by rendering the beef fat and cooking the flour in it for 2 minutes. Remove from the heat and gradually stir in the wine and stock mixture to form a

smooth sauce. Simmer very gently for 20 minutes.

4 Season the steaks lightly with salt and generously with freshly ground black pepper. Pour the sauce over them and garnish with chopped parsley. Serve immediately.

Serves 4

Steak Manzanilla

2 rump steaks, about ½ lb. each
2 tablespoons oil
salt and pepper
2 slices Cheddar cheese, ⅛ inch
  thick
pinch paprika
4 anchovy fillets
2 stuffed green olives, sliced

1 Brush the steaks with oil and season with a little salt and plenty of freshly ground black pepper. Broil the steaks under high heat for 3-4 minutes on each side according to taste.

2 Place a slice of cheese on each steak, sprinkle with paprika and broil until the cheese is melted and just starting to brown.

3 Place the steaks on a warm serving dish. Decorate each steak with anchovy fillets, and slices of stuffed olive. Serve immediately.

Serves 2

Steak à l'Orange

4 sirloin steaks, ¾ inch thick
24 black peppercorns, crushed
rind 1 orange, cut in matchstick
  strips
1 tablespoon oil
⅔ cup dry sherry

Steak Manzanilla is an unusual dish featuring cheese and anchovies, which would also suit cheaper cuts of steak

4 fresh mint leaves
⅔ cup light cream

For the Marinade:
juice 2 oranges
2 cloves garlic, peeled and crushed
1 teaspoon fresh gingerroot, finely
  chopped
2 tablespoons soy sauce
¼ cup oil
2 tablespoons cider vinegar

1 Trim the steaks and rub the crushed black peppercorns into them.

2 Thoroughly blend the orange juice, garlic, ginger, soy sauce, oil, and vinegar to make a marinade. Soak the steaks in it for 20 minutes and then remove them, reserving the marinade.

3 Meanwhile, boil the orange rind for 8 minutes. Drain and rinse the strips in cold water and add them to the leftover marinade.

4 Fry the steaks in the oil until done to taste. Remove and keep warm. Pour the marinade into the pan and boil for 4 minutes to reduce. Add the sherry and mint leaves and boil for 3 minutes; then stir in the cream and boil 3 more minutes. Pour the sauce over the steaks and serve at once.

Serves 4

Sirloin with Peppercorns and Garlic

four ¾-lb. sirloin steaks, 1 inch
 thick
12 black peppercorns
4 cloves garlic, thinly sliced
⅓ cup oil
salt

1 Trim the fat from the steaks. Crush the peppercorns, using a rolling pin, and then sprinkle over both sides of the steaks, pressing well into the meat.

2 Make several slits in the surface of the steaks and insert the slices of garlic into the slits. Brush the steaks with oil and then cook them under a broiler, over a charcoal fire, or in a skillet. Cook for 2 minutes on both sides for rare meat, 4 minutes for medium or 8 minutes for well-done.

3 Season with salt and serve with watercress, French fries and a pat of garlic butter.

Serves 4

Rump Steak Royal

2-lb. rump steak in 1 piece
salt
1 teaspoon crushed peppercorns
3 tablespoons oil

Sirloin with Peppercorns and Garlic — try this deliciously different way of serving your steaks

2 cloves garlic, peeled and
 chopped
¼ cup peanut butter
⅔ cup dry vermouth

1 Season the steak with salt and peppercorns.

2 Heat the oil in a skillet and fry the steak. Cook for 6 minutes on either side for rare meat, 12 minutes for medium, 14 minutes for well-done.

3 Remove the steak from the pan and keep warm on a dish.

4 Mix the garlic and peanut butter and put in the skillet. Add the vermouth, stir and boil for 4 minutes. Pour over the steak.

5 Serve the steak whole and cut into 3 or 4 portions in front of the guests. Serve with a lettuce and orange salad.

Serves 3–4

Pineapple Barbecue Sauce

⅔ cup pineapple juice
2 tablespoons soy sauce
1 tablespoon Worcestershire sauce
3 cloves garlic, peeled and
  chopped
1 tablespoon freshly peeled gingerroot, chopped
1 small onion
2 tablespoons vinegar
1 tablespoon honey
pinch salt
pinch cayenne pepper

For the Stock:
½ cup water
1 beef bouillon cube
1½ tablespoons cornstarch
⅓ cup water

For the Garnish:
1 tablespoon pineapple pieces

1 Blend the ingredients and marinate the steaks to be barbecued for 30 minutes.

2 When the steaks are removed, add the water and beef bouillon cube; boil the marinade for 5 minutes.

3 Thicken with the cornstarch mixed with the water.

4 Add the garnish, reheat and pour over the steaks or serve separately.

Makes 1¼ cups

Hot Chili Tomato Sauce

This and the following recipe are delicious sauces to serve with barbecued steaks

¼ cup tomato paste
2 cloves garlic, peeled and
  chopped
1 green chili, seeded, sliced
1 red chili, seeded, sliced

Dip barbecued beef into tangy Hot Chili Tomato Sauce, Pineapple Barbecue Sauce or Mushroom & Sour Cream Sauce

1 onion, chopped
2 tablespoons vinegar
2 tablespoons soy sauce
1 tablespoon sugar
⅔ cup water
1 tablespoon oil
1 chicken bouillon cube
pinch salt, oregano and basil

To thicken the Sauce:
1½ tablespoons cornstarch
⅓ cup water

For the Garnish:
4 tomatoes, skinned, seeded and
  chopped
2 tablespoons corn kernels,
  cooked or canned

1 Blend all the ingredients and marinate the steaks to be barbecued for 30 minutes.

2 When the steaks are removed, boil the marinade for 4 minutes.

3 Mix the cornstarch with the water and add to the marinade. Boil for 1 minute to thicken.

4 Add the garnish and reheat. Pour over the steaks, or serve separately.

Makes 1¼ cups

Tournedos with Anchovy Butter

6 slices lean bacon (blanched)
6 tournedos steaks, ¼ lb. each,
  1½ inches thick
salt and freshly ground pepper
oil for frying steaks
6 green olives
6 anchovy fillets
2 tablespoons catsup

For the Anchovy Butter:
¼ lb. butter
1 tablespoon chopped parsley
juice ½ lemon
4 anchovy fillets, finely chopped
6 slices bread
2 tablespoons butter
2 tablespoons oil

1 Prepare the anchovy butter by creaming the butter with the parsley, lemon juice and anchovy fillets to form a paste. Roll the paste into a cylinder, wrap in parchment paper, and chill for 1 hour.

2 Make the croûtons by cutting six bread circles using a plain cutter of 2½ inches. Put the butter and oil in a skillet and fry the bread on both sides until golden. Place the croûtons on a dish and keep warm.

3 Tie a slice of lean bacon around each steak and season. Heat some oil in the skillet and fry the steaks for 4-10 minutes, depending on whether you want the steaks rare, medium or well-done. If preferred, brush the steaks with oil, and broil. Remove the bacon. Place on the croûtons.

4 When ready to serve, cut slices off the roll of anchovy butter and place one on each steak. Place a green olive on each, surrounded by an anchovy fillet, and trickle a little catsup around as decoration. Serve at once with thin French fries as illustrated.

Serves 6

Tournedos with Anchovy Butter combines succulent steak with piquant anchovies, topped with green olives

Steak Mignonette

4 slices of ¼ lb. tenderloin steak, cut from the thin end as for a Filet Mignon

200

1 medium onion
2 tablespoons butter
4 mushrooms
$\frac{2}{3}$ cup port
2 tablespoons tomato paste
pinch thyme
pinch cinnamon
$\frac{1}{3}$ cup light cream
salt and pepper
2 tablespoons oil
8 stuffed olives, sliced

1 Flatten the steaks to $5 \times 2\frac{1}{2}$ inches.

2 Chop the onion and sauté gently in the butter for 4 minutes until tender, without coloring. Chop the mushrooms and add, and cook for 1 minute. Then add the port, tomato paste, thyme and cinnamon. Boil for 5 minutes. Stir in the cream, season and put aside. Keep warm.

3 Heat the oil in a skillet. Quickly cook the steaks for 1 minute on each side.

4 Put in a dish, pour half of the sauce over the steaks and sprinkle with the sliced stuffed olives. Serve the remainder of the sauce separately. Serve garnished with braised endive.

Serves 4

Brandy Steak with Mandarin Rice

$\frac{3}{4}$ cup long grain rice
salt and pepper
2 tablespoons butter
11 ozs. canned mandarin oranges
4 tenderloin steaks, $\frac{1}{4}$ lb. each,
  $1\frac{1}{2}$ inches thick
4 slices lean bacon (blanched)
2 tablespoons butter
2 tablespoons oil
4 tablespoons brandy
$\frac{1}{2}$ cup light cream

Brandy Steak with Mandarin Rice; tender tournedos are flamed in brandy and flavored with mandarin oranges

1 Wash the rice and cook in salted boiling water for 20 minutes. Drain, and stir in the butter. Season and keep warm.

2 Meanwhile, heat the mandarin oranges in their syrup and drain. Keep the juice. Add the oranges to the rice. Keep warm.

3 Season the steaks, and tie a slice of bacon around each. Heat the butter and oil in a skillet, and shallow fry the steaks for 2-3 minutes on each side, if you like them rare. Cook longer if you prefer. If you want the steaks well done, put a lid on the pan.

4 Pour the brandy into the skillet and flame the steaks. Remove the steaks, discard the bacon, and put them on a dish and keep warm.

5 Pour the cream into the skillet, and mix with the meat juices, and boil for 2 minutes to make a smooth sauce. Remove from the heat, add 1 tablespoon of the mandarin juice and pour over the steaks. Serve at once with the mandarin rice, and a green salad.

Serves 4

Hamburger Steaks

Hamburgers are quick, tasty and universally popular. The traditional American hamburger is lean ground beef, lightly shaped, then grilled, broiled or fried — but you may bind it with egg and breadcrumbs, and flavor it with a few drops of a piquant sauce, a pinch of herbs or minced onion. For best results, pass the meat through a grinder twice. Always use lean beef from a cut you would otherwise pot roast or braise, such as flank or chuck.

Beefsteak à la Lindstrom

1 lb. lean ground beef
1 onion, finely chopped
4 sprigs parsley, chopped
1 tablespoon capers
1 cooked beet, chopped
1 hard-boiled egg
1 egg, beaten
good pinch salt
pinch white pepper
pinch sugar
¾ cup dried breadcumbs
3 tablespoons oil

1 In a large mixing bowl, combine the ground beef, onion, chopped parsley, capers and chopped beef. Mash the hard-boiled egg with a fork and add it. Mix together well and knead.

2 Blend the beaten egg into the mixture with a spoon and season with salt, pepper and sugar.

3 Divide the mixture into 4 balls, then flatten them slightly. Place the breadcrumbs on a plate. Coat the cakes evenly with them.

4 Heat the oil in a skillet and fry the cakes for 5 minutes on each side. Serve hot.

Serves 4

Beefsteak à la Lindstrom is a hamburger with a difference, containing piquant capers and chopped beet

South Seas Meatballs

1 lb. lean ground beef
1 beaten egg
pinch each salt and pepper
1 tablespoon oil
3 shallots, minced
2 tablespoons flour
1 lb. pineapple chunks
1 tablespoon soy sauce
1 teaspoon wine vinegar
½ green pepper, finely chopped
¼ cup almonds, blanched

1 In a large bowl blend the beef, beaten egg, salt and pepper. Make into 4 flattened balls, brush with oil and broil for 10 minutes, turning once. Keep warm.

2 Heat the oil in a skillet. Add the shallots and sauté gently for 3 minutes. Take out. Stir in the flour and cook the roux for 3 minutes more. Pour in the juice from the canned pineapple, and bring to a boil, stirring. Add the soy sauce and vinegar. Season to taste.

3 Add the shallots, pineapple chunks, green pepper and almonds. Place the meatballs in the pan and heat through, spooning on the sauce.

Serves 4

South Seas Meatballs have a sweet-sour fruity flavor, and make a tasty supper for the family

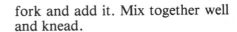

Marengo Meatballs

1 large slice white bread
2 tablespoons milk
1½ lbs. lean ground beef
1 egg yolk
1 onion, finely chopped
pinch salt and pepper
1 tablespoon flour
¼ cup butter
⅓ cup dry white wine
4 large tomatoes, skinned,
  seeded and chopped
pinch sugar
1½ cups long grain rice
2 tablespoons light cream
1 tablespoon chopped parsley

1 Soak the bread in the milk for 5 minutes. Squeeze out, remove excess liquid and crumble into breadcrumbs.

2 In a mixing bowl, combine the beef, egg yolk, onion, salt and pepper and breadcrumbs. Divide into 6 and roll into flattened balls. Dust with the flour.

3 Heat the butter in a skillet and fry the meatballs for 10 minutes, turning them once. Pour on the wine, then add the tomatoes and a pinch of sugar. Bring to a boil, then reduce the heat and simmer for 25 minutes.

4 Meanwhile, place the rice in a pan of slightly salted water. Bring to a boil and cook for 15 minutes or until the rice is just tender. Drain. Heat the cream in a small pan and pour over the rice. Sprinkle with the parsley and arrange in the center of a serving dish surrounded by the meatballs and sauce.

Serves 6

Margeno Meatballs use ground beef with creamy rice for a nourishing and economical meal

Mushroom Burgers

2 tablespoons butter
2 tablespoons oil
2 onions, finely chopped
2 cups finely chopped mushrooms
pinch mixed herbs
1 clove garlic, peeled and crushed
1½ lbs. lean ground beef
pinch salt and pepper
2 tablespoons flour

1 Heat the butter and 1 tablespoon oil in a skillet. Gently fry the onions and the mushrooms for 5 minutes. Add the mixed herbs and the crushed garlic clove and cook for a further minute. Allow to cool.

2 In a bowl, combine the beef with the onion and mushroom mixture. Season. Divide into 8 balls, then flatten slightly. Dust with the flour.

3 Heat the rest of the oil in the pan and fry the mushroom burgers slowly for 4-6 minutes on each side.

Serves 4

Tip: To make a quick, tasty sauce, take the burgers out of the pan when they are cooked and keep hot. Pour away the oil and add ½ cup sherry, wine or fruit juice to the pan. Boil rapidly until the sauce is reduced by half and pour it over the burgers.

Mushroom Burgers are tasty and easy to make. Serve them with a big mixed salad and French fries

Meatballs with Zucchini

⅓ cup chickpeas, canned
 and drained
1 lb. lean ground beef
1 clove garlic, peeled and crushed
1 cup fresh breadcrumbs
⅓ cup hazelnuts, finely chopped
1 egg, beaten
1 small green seeded chili pepper,
 finely chopped
1 tablespoon chopped parsley
pinch cumin
salt and pepper
2 tablespoons flour
¼ cup oil

For the Sauce:
2 tablespoons oil
1 onion, chopped
1 clove garlic, peeled and crushed
4 zucchini, sliced
4 tomatoes, skinned, seeded
 and chopped

*Meatballs with Zucchini includes
other unusual vegetables —
chickpeas, hot chili pepper
and hazelnuts*

1¼ cups peas, fresh or frozen
1¼ cups water
1 chicken bouillon cube
1 tablespoon mixed mint and
 parsley, chopped

1 Preheat the oven to 400°F.

2 Mash the chickpeas with a fork.
Place them in a mixing bowl, and
add the beef, garlic, breadcrumbs,
hazelnuts, beaten egg and chili pepper. Blend together well and add
the parsley, cumin, salt and pepper.
Shape into 8 slightly flattened balls
and dust with the flour.

3 Heat the oil in a skillet and fry
the meatballs for 6-8 minutes.
Drain and keep hot.

4 To make the sauce, pour off the
oil in which the meatballs were
cooked and wipe the pan clean.
Heat 2 tablespoons oil and gently
sauté the onion for 4 minutes, until
soft but not brown. Add the garlic,
zucchini, tomatoes and peas. Pour
on the water and crumble in the
bouillon cube. Bring to a boil, add
the parsley and mint and season to
taste. Transfer to a casserole, add
the meatballs, and place in the oven
for 20 minutes.

Serves 4

Tips: Try using equal quantities of
ground pork and beef for a good
texture as well as a delicious flavor.

For economy, replace ½ cup ground
meat with 2½ ozs. texturized vegetable protein.

Meatballs can be braised in the
oven or deep fried and any kind of
cereal binder can be used, such as
matzo meal, oats, cooked rice.

Steak Tartare

Steak Tartare is the name given to a delicious, unusual and highly digestible dish of raw steak.

You should use tenderloin steak — preferably the thin, tail end — but you can use sirloin or rib, both of which are very tender. Make sure the meat is absolutely fresh: locally killed beef is best. Allow ¼ lb. meat for a generous portion per person, and make sure it is passed through a grinder twice.

1 lb. ground tenderloin steak
salt and freshly ground pepper
½ cup shallots, finely chopped
2 tablespoons chopped parsley

8 anchovy fillets, chopped
1 tablespoon capers
1 tablespoon chopped dill pickle
few pearl onions
⅔ cup vinaigrette sauce
⅔ cup mayonnaise
4 eggs

1 Season the ground steak with salt and freshly ground black pepper. Divide it into 4 portions and shape each into a ball. Place each in the center of a dinner plate, flatten slightly and make a small cavity in the center.

Steak Tartare is a classic dish in which diners garnish raw tenderloin steak according to their individual tastes

2 Either surround each portion with, or serve separately, the shallots, parsley, anchovy fillets, capers, dill pickles and pearl onions. Serve a bowl each of vinaigrette sauce and mayonnaise.

3 Carefully break each egg and separate the white from the yolk. Leave the yolk in half the shell and place in the center of each steak.

4 Allow your guests to help themselves to the various garnishes and sauces.

Serves 4

Tip: Serve Tartare with a crisp salad. Try lettuce and Belgian endive, or potato or orange and watercress or Waldorf Salad, which combines celery, crisp apples and walnuts.

Roast Beef

There are two methods of roasting beef. The old-fashioned method roasts the meat at a high temperature. This sears the outside of the roast and keeps the meat juices inside. The moisture acts as a heat conductor and so the roast stays moist and juicy long after cooking. Lovers of rare beef also claim that it has more flavor this way. An alternative is to start the cooking on a high temperature and sear the roast for 20 minutes, then lower the temperature for the remainder of the cooking time.

The second method roasts the meat at a low temperature. This way, the meat is cooked through and it is difficult to obtain a rare, juicy, red roast. You will probably find it best to sear your roast first, then lower the temperature.

Basic rules for Roasting

There are some basic rules for roasting and, if you follow them, you should always have good results. They are:

1 Always handle the meat very gently and never pierce it with a knife or skewer. It is important that the meat juices should stay intact.

2 Always smother your meat with plenty of fat — a mixture of butter and lard is best. Use 2 tablespoons fat for every 1 lb. meat. Baste the meat frequently with the fat during cooking.

3 If you can, stand the roast on a rack or trivet above a roasting pan to catch the juices. An alternative is to place the roast on a bed of root vegetables (carrots, celery and onions) or meat bones. The vegetable and meat juices can be used as a base for the gravy.

4 Always use a meat thermometer if you like your meat well-done. It is essential to obtain good results. Insert it into the meat but take care that it does not touch the bone.

5 Always preheat the oven before roasting to 425°F. Cook the meat on the middle shelf and sear it at the high temperature. Then, if you like your beef rare, continue cooking it at this temperature. If you prefer well-done beef, lower the temperature to 375°F.

Serving Roast Beef

The traditional way to serve roast beef is with roast potatoes, Yorkshire pudding and horseradish sauce and mustard. You can make a delicious gravy from the meat juices and vegetable water. Let the roast cool for 10 minutes before carving and garnish with sprigs of watercress.

Suitable Cuts of Meat

Sirloin, rib or short loin, forerib and middlerib are all suitable for roasting. If these are too expensive, try chuck or round which are cheaper and slightly tougher cuts.

Roasting Times

Sirloin, rib and the better cuts of beef should be seared for 20 minutes in a hot oven. Then, if you like your meat rare, roast it a further 10 minutes for every 1 lb. For well cooked meat, allow 15-20 minutes per lb. Chuck and the cheaper cuts need 20 minutes also.

Yorkshire Pudding

2 eggs
1¼ cups flour, sifted
1¼ cups water, or milk and water mixed
pinch salt

1 Beat the eggs well, then stir in the flour. Add the liquid and beat for 3 to 4 minutes to obtain a smooth batter. Season with the salt.

2 If your oven is not already hot, preheat it to 375°F.

3 Place a teaspoonful of the meat fat and juices in the bottom of each muffin tin and heat in the oven for 5 minutes. Then half-fill them with batter and bake for 15-20 minutes until well-risen and golden. The pudding may also be cooked in a Pyrex casserole. Use 3 tablespoons of meat fat and preheat the casserole before adding the batter.

Makes 6–8

Horseradish Sauce

3 ozs. fresh horseradish root, peeled and washed
3 tablespoons wine vinegar
salt and pepper
pinch sugar
1¼ cups milk
1½ cups fresh white breadcrumbs

1 Grate the horseradish and soak in the wine vinegar for 1 hour. Season with the salt and pepper and sugar.

2 Heat the milk in a saucepan and bring to a boil. Stir in the breadcrumbs and leave them to soak for 10 minutes. Blend in the horseradish mixture and serve the sauce with roast beef.

Makes about 1¼ cups

Tip: For a change, try making horseradish sauce in the Hungarian way. Just mix the horseradish and vinegar mixture into 1¼ cups white sauce.

Roast Rib of Beef, served with Yorkshire Pudding and Horseradish Sauce, is a meal fit for a king

CHEF'S CHOICE
Boeuf en Brioche

The main characteristic of this dish is that the meat is cooked wrapped in pastry. Originally a bread dough was used, but over the years this has changed and a brioche dough or puff pastry is now used.

The basic method is that the meat is first browned in hot fat to seal in the juices and, when cold, wrapped in pastry and baked.

The most famous version of this dish is Beef Wellington, created in honor of the Duke of Wellington after his victory over Napoleon at the Battle of Waterloo. For this the finest meat was chosen — a tenderloin of beef.

The French decided to commemorate the loser, and created Beef Napoleon. In this dish, the sealed tenderloin was spread with foie gras (goose liver) and rolled in chopped truffles, and then wrapped in brioche pastry and baked.

We show you a plain version, leaving you to choose your own flavored paste. Here is a suggestion which will add a touch of distinction — spread the sealed meat with liver pâté mixed with freshly chopped mushrooms, before wrapping it up in the brioche dough.

The finest quality meat is chosen for this dish. In England it is called a fillet, in the United States a tenderloin.

Boeuf en Brioche

2½-lb. tenderloin wrapped in bacon
  or pork fat
salt and pepper
⅓ cup oil
1 egg, beaten

For the Brioche Dough:
6¾ cups all-purpose flour
2 teaspoons salt
½ oz. compressed fresh yeast
⅔ cup warm water
4 eggs
¾ cup soft butter

1 Sift the flour and salt onto a board. Put ¼ of the flour to one side, making two circles.

2 Crumble the yeast into the warm water, and place in the small circle. Mix in the flour, put in a bowl, sprinkle with more flour and put in a warm place for 30 minutes.

3 Break the eggs into the well of the larger circle and mix in the flour to a soft dough, using your fingertips. Beat with an up and down yo-yo-like motion for 6-7 minutes until the dough is firmer and no longer sticks to your fingers.

4 Mix the yeast dough with the egg dough and give the mixture a thorough beating.

5 Mix in the soft butter in small pieces. Put the dough in a bread bowl, cover with a cloth and allow to proof and rise for 45 minutes.

6 Preheat the oven to 425°F.

7 Meanwhile, season the tenderloin. Heat the oil in a skillet and brown the meat all over for 5 minutes with the lid on. Transfer the meat and oil to a roasting pan and roast in the oven for 15-35 minutes. Cool. Remove the bacon.

8 Grease a baking sheet.

9 When the meat is cold, knead the dough for 5 minutes. Roll out to ¼ inch thick. Place the meat in the middle and brush with beaten egg. (Add flavored pastes at this stage if you wish.) Brush the dough with beaten egg and fold over the meat, making a large overlap. Turn the roast over so that the seam is underneath. Trim off both ends and shape into a loaf.

10 Roll out the trimmings and cut into thin strips. Brush the loaf with beaten egg, arrange the strips and brush again. Place on the greased baking sheet.

11 Preheat the oven to 425°F.

12 Allow the loaf to proof for 25 minutes so that the brioche dough may rise. Prick in two or three places.

13 Bake on the middle shelf of the oven for 15 minutes, then reduce the temperature to 375°F. for another 20 minutes. Watch the pastry so that it does not burn.

14 Remove from the oven and cool for 10 minutes before carving. Cut in 1-inch slices. Serve with a brown sauce flavored with Madeira or sherry.

Serves 8

Tip: The success of this dish depends on cooking the tenderloin at the beginning for the right amount of time to rare, medium or well-done. When the dough is wrapped around, no further heat will penetrate the meat and only the pastry will be cooked.

Variation

If you wish to make the classic Beef Wellington, spread the prepared tenderloin with the following mixture. Chop ½ lb. mushrooms and 1 onion, and mix with ⅓ cup of diced ham. Put in a skillet with ½ cup of breadcrumbs and sauté for 5 minutes in 1 oz. of oil. Then add ½ cup ground chicken livers and stir. When the mixture has cooled, add 4 tablespoons butter and a beaten egg, seasoning and 1 teaspoon of chopped fresh parsley.

You will see that the meat shrinks slightly during the baking, and the pastry expands, leaving a gap between. If you use a flavored spread like this, the gap is filled, and the dish enhanced by the extra flavors that you have added.

Boeuf en Brioche combines simplicity with excellence — a delicious loin of beef, cooked in light pastry

1 Make two circles of sifted flour. Mix the yeast with water, pour into the smaller circle and mix with the flour 2 Put the yeast mixture into a small bowl in a warm place to rise. Break the eggs into the larger circle 3 Gradually mix the flour to a soft dough using the fingertips 4 Beat with an up and down, yo-yo like motion for 5-6 minutes until the dough no longer sticks to your fingers 5 Mix in the soft butter in small pieces. Cover with a cloth and leave to proof for 45 minutes 6 Heat the oil in a skillet and add the seasoned tender-

loin **7** Brown all over for 5 minutes to seal the juices, with a lid on. Roast in the oven for 15 minutes at 425°F. and then cool **8** Roll out the dough ¼ inch thick **9** Place the cold tenderloin in the center and brush with beaten egg. (Add flavored pastes at this stage if you wish). **10** Brush the dough with beaten egg and fold over the fillet **11** Fold over the other half making a large overlap, and turn over so that the seam is underneath **12** Trim off each end, sealing the tenderloin inside **13** Form into a loaf shape **14** Roll out the trim-

mings and cut into strips. Brush the loaf with beaten egg **15** Arrange the strips decoratively **16** Brush them with beaten egg and place on a baking sheet and proof for 25 minutes. Prick in two or three places **17** Bake for 15 minutes at 425°F. and for 20 minutes at 375°F. Watch the pastry so that it does not burn. Remove from the oven and cool for 10 minutes **18** Carve in 1-inch slices and serve hot

Beef Italienne

1½-lb. tenderloin
4 strips bacon
⅓ cup oil
1 carrot, 1 onion and 2 celery
  branches, sliced

For the Gravy:
⅔ cup white wine
1 cup water
1 beef bouillon cube
bouquet garni
1 teaspoon cornstarch

1 Prepare the tenderloin by removing the tough skin carefully with a knife to avoid damaging the meat. Lay the bacon along the tenderloin and secure with string, tied at intervals of 1 inch.

2 Preheat the oven to 400°F.

3 Heat the oil in a skillet and brown the meat all over for 8 minutes to seal.

4 Transfer the meat to a roasting pan and add the carrot, onion and celery.

5 Roast for 40 minutes. Remove from the oven, discard the bacon, string, and vegetables. Place on a serving dish and keep hot.

6 To the juices in the roasting pan, add the wine, ⅔ cup water, bouillon cube, and bouquet garni and simmer for 15 minutes. Thicken with cornstarch mixed with the remaining water. Boil for 3 minutes, season and strain.

Serves 6

Beef Italienne could be the star attraction at a special dinner — superb tenderloin, flamboyantly garnished

Tip: As the photograph shows, the Beef Italienne may be garnished in several ways.

With small strips of fresh noodle dough deep fried until crisp and golden and arranged in heaps around the dish.

With globe artichokes, boiled in water and lemon juice, after the outside leaves and hairy choke have been removed. The artichokes may be filled with a duxelles of ham, mushrooms, onion and breadcrumbs, sautéed for 5 minutes.

The dish may be decorated with a few mushrooms, which have been scribed with the point of a knife blade, and then blanched in water with lemon juice or wine.

The garnishes should be prepared before the meat is cooked.

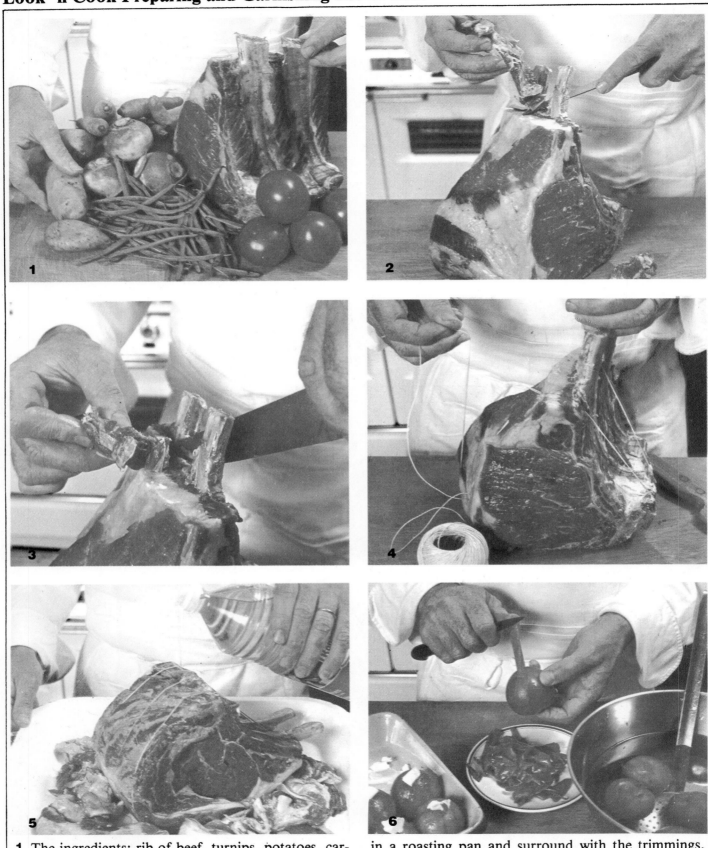

1 The ingredients: rib of beef, turnips, potatoes, carrots, green beans and tomatoes 2 and 3 Trim the rib for roasting. Expose the ends of the bones and remove the fat and trimmings. Reserve for use later 4 Tie the rib with trussing string to keep its shape 5 Place the rib in a roasting pan and surround with the trimmings, which will provide the gravy. Season lightly and pour on a little oil 6 Scald and skin the tomatoes. Place them in a greased ovenproof dish and dot with butter 7 Peel the carrots, turnips and potatoes and trim them

7

8

9

10

11

12

to a uniform size **8** Put each vegetable into a separate pan. Pour on enough water to cover and add a little butter and a pinch each salt and sugar. Cover, and put on to boil **9, 10** and **11** When the vegetables are tender, reduce the water in which they were cooked and glaze them with the sugar and butter. Brown the potatoes in a sauté pan with a little more butter **12** The finished dish: roast rib of beef, surrounded by vegetables, ready to carve and serve

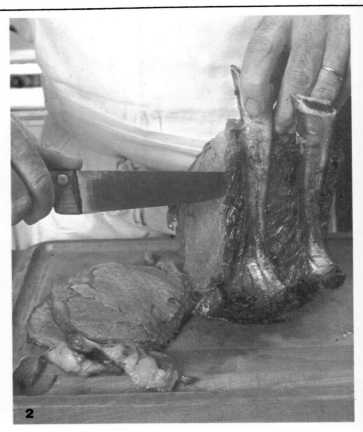

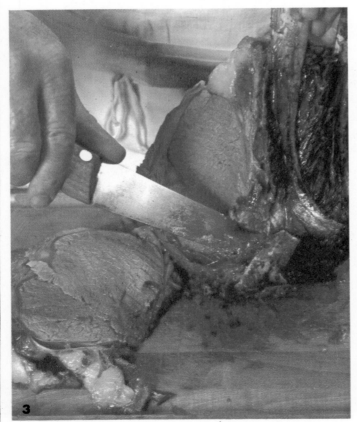

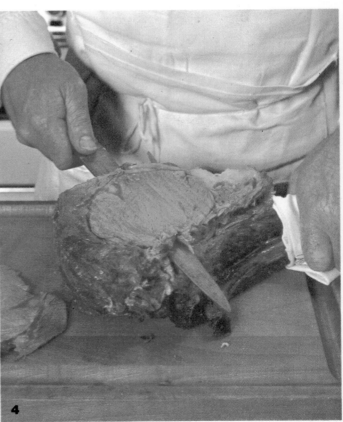

Beef ribs can be carved in two ways, vertically or horizontally **1** To carve vertically, hold the ribs upright on their base and cut regular slices until the knife meets the first bone **2** Start to remove the first bone by sliding the blade of the knife down between the bone and the meat **3** Complete the removal **4** To carve horizontally, place the ribs flat and slice from the thickest part of the roast **5** Continue until the knife reaches the nar-

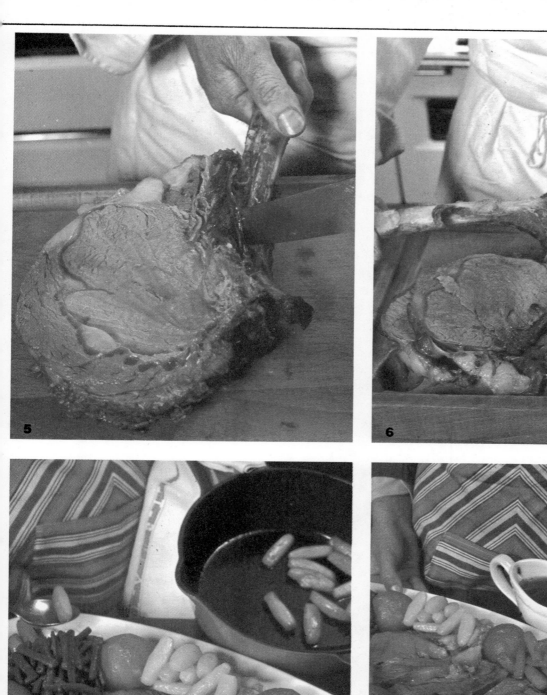

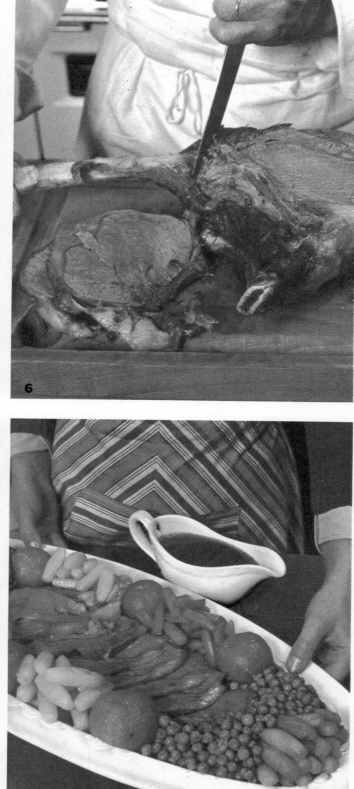

5

6

7

8

row part and then the first bone. Cut out the bone by running the blade of the knife around it **6** Bend the bone back to separate it from the meat **7** Put the slices on the serving dish. Surround them with the vegetables such as those illustrated here **8** The completed dish with the sauce boat of gravy, peas, carrots, potatoes and tomatoes

Braised Beef

Braised meat is first seared in hot fat to seal in the juices, and then barely covered with a water-based liquid and cooked gently until tender. For additional flavor, the meat can be soaked in a marinade before it is cooked; the marinade liquid should always include vinegar, wine or fruit juice for the best flavor.

Beef Olives with Ham

4 thin slices of braising steak, ¼ lb. each, from leg or shoulder
4 thin slices cooked ham
1 small onion, chopped
1 clove garlic, chopped
few sage leaves, chopped
2 tablespoons chopped parsley
salt and pepper
¼ lb. butter

Beef Olives with Ham uses a less expensive beef dressed up with a garnish of mushrooms and onions

½ cup oil
1 onion, coarsely chopped
1 carrot, coarsely chopped
1 tablespoon flour
⅔ cup red wine
1¼ cups brown stock
1 tablespoon capers
⅔ cup long grain rice
2 cups pearl onions
½ lb. mushrooms

1 Preheat the oven to 350°F.

2 Beat the steaks until very thin. Place a slice of ham on each steak. Mix together the chopped onion, garlic, sage and half the parsley and divide the mixture between the steaks. Sprinkle with salt and pepper.

3 Roll up the steaks tightly and secure with string or toothpicks.

4 Heat 2½ tablespoons of the butter and half the oil together in a pan, add the meat and fry briskly for 5 minutes.

5 Transfer the meat to a casserole dish. Add the chopped vegetables to the pan, and sauté gently, covered, for about 8 minutes or until soft. Sprinkle in the flour and cook for 1-2 minutes or until brown. Stir in the wine and stock and bring to a boil. Pour the contents of the pan over the meat, add the capers and season to taste. Cover the dish and cook in the oven for 1¼ hours.

6 Meanwhile, prepare the garnish. Boil the rice in salted water for 18 minutes, drain and blend in 4 tablespoons of the butter and salt and pepper. Heat the rest of the oil and butter in a pan and sauté the onions for 3 minutes until brown. Add the mushrooms and cook for 1 minute more. Cover the vegetables with water and boil for 6 minutes. Drain.

7 When the meat is cooked, arrange the rice on a warm serving dish, place the meat on top and garnish with the mushrooms and onions, and the rest of the parsley.

Serves 4

Braised Beef Home-Style

**2 lbs. braising beef from leg, in
  1 piece**
1 onion, finely sliced
**1 clove garlic, peeled and
  quartered**
bouquet garni
$\frac{1}{4}$ cup brandy
1$\frac{1}{4}$ cups dry white wine
$\frac{1}{4}$ lb. butter
2 onions, chopped
$\frac{7}{8}$ cup stock
pinch mixed spice
salt and pepper
1 lb. carrots, sliced
1 lb. green beans

*Braised Beef Home-Style provides
a hearty mixture of lean beef and
vegetables to satisfy a hungry
family*

1 Place the meat in a bowl, and
add the sliced onion, garlic, bouquet garni, brandy and two-thirds
of the wine. Leave to marinate for 3
hours.
2 Drain the meat, reserving the
marinade, and dry. Melt half the
butter in a flameproof casserole,
add the meat and fry briskly until
browned all over. Add the chopped
onion and fry until golden-brown.
Strain the reserved marinade and
add it to the pan with the stock,
mixed spice and salt and pepper to

taste. Cover and cook gently for 2
hours.
3 Melt the remaining butter in a
separate pan, add the carrots and
fry gently until browned. Add just
enough water to cover, then cook
gently until the carrots are tender.
Cook the beans in salted water until
tender, then drain.
4 When the meat is cooked, add
the vegetables to the casserole,
cover and cook for a further 15
minutes.
5 Drain the meat and carve into
neat slices. Arrange on a warm
serving dish and surround with the
vegetables and gravy. Serve hot
with roast potatoes.
Serves 6

221

13

14

15

16

1 The ingredients **2** and **3** Push the larding needle through the beef, thread the strip of fat through the needle and draw back through the meat **4** and **5** Add to the beef the vegetables, garlic, bouquet garni, peppercorns, brandy and wine. Soak for 2 hours **6** Strain, reserving the liquid **7** Brown the beef and remove **8** Sauté the vegetables and herbs **9** Return the beef to the pan with the calves feet, reserved liquid and stock **10** Bring to a boil, remove any scum and place in the oven. Glaze the onions and carrots **11** After 1½ hours, transfer the beef to another casserole. Dice the meat from the calves feet and add **12** Add the glazed carrots and onions **13** Strain over ¾ of the gravy and complete the cooking **14** Reduce (evaporate) the rest of the gravy and use to glaze the cooked beef **15** and **16** Serve the beef with the vegetables and the juices left in the casserole

Boeuf à la Mode

1 lb. salt pork
salt and pepper
2 tablespoons chopped parsley
4½ lbs. braising beef
2½ cups red wine
bouquet garni
1½ lbs. carrots
1 shallot, sliced
2 large onions, sliced
2 cloves garlic, crushed
6 peppercorns
¼ cup brandy
½ cup oil
2 calves feet, cut in half (optional)
4¼ cups beef stock
¼ lb. butter
1 teaspoon sugar
12 pearl onions
3 tablespoons cornstarch mixed
   with ⅔ cup water (optional)

1 Cut the pork fat into strips, ½ inch thick. Season and sprinkle on the parsley. Lard the beef at regular intervals with the strips (see pages 222-223).

2 Place the meat in an earthenware dish with the wine and bouquet garni. Cut half the carrots in slices across and add them to the dish with the shallot, onions, garlic, peppercorns and brandy. Leave in the refrigerator for 2 hours, turning from time to time.

3 Preheat the oven to 350°F. Strain the meat and vegetables, reserving the liquid. Heat the oil in an oven-proof casserole, add the beef and cook quickly for 10 minutes until browned. Lift out the meat and sauté the strained vegetables and bouquet garni for 5 minutes.

4 Return the beef to the pan, add the calves' feet and pour in the reserved liquid and the beef stock. Season and bring to a boil. Remove any scum, cover the dish and cook in the oven for 2-2½ hours.

5 Heat half the butter in a pan, add the rest of the carrots, the sugar and enough water to cover. Cook until the liquid has evaporated. In a separate pan, heat the rest of the butter, add the onions and enough water to cover and cook for 8 minutes.

6 After the meat has been cooking for 1½ hours, remove from the oven and transfer the beef to another casserole. Dice the meat of the calves' feet and discard the bones. Add the diced meat to the beef with the glazed carrots and onions. Strain the gravy and add about three-quarters to the beef. Cover again and return to the oven for the rest of the cooking time.

7 Boil the rest of the gravy for 5 minutes to reduce it. Season.

As a variation of Boeuf à la Mode, chuck may be braised in stout instead of wine. This gives it a darker color and a rich malty flavor. It may be served cold in its gravy

8 Place the cooked meat on a serving dish and coat with the reduced gravy. Return to the oven for a few minutes to glaze.

9 Surround the meat with the vegetables, coat with the gravy and serve hot. The gravy can be thickened with flour if liked.

Serves 8

All about
Beef Stews and
Casseroles

Daube of Beef in Red Wine

Beef Stews

Stews and casseroles provide the best methods of cooking tougher cuts of beef. They all involve slow cooking at a low heat with a measured volume of liquid: (that is, one cup meat to one cup liquid) although you can use a pressure cooker. You can use a covered pan on the stove and simmer at 180°F. but for best results, cook in a casserole in an oven preheated to 350°F.

The cooking liquor should be slightly acid, to help tenderize the meat. Include a little wine, cider, beer, tomato paste or fruit juice. The meat can be marinated first, and the marinade included in the cooking liquor. For a better flavor, fry the meat quickly in fat to brown it and seal in the juices. Root vegetables and onions which are added for flavor should be lightly fried, too, before you add stock and any aromatic herbs you may wish to include. Flour for thickening can be added when the meat is browned, or as a roux stirred into the cooking liquor when the stew is nearly done. A stew cooked with beans makes a meal in itself.

Cuts suitable for stewing come from muscular areas, such as leg and shoulder. Rump steak, top round, flank, skirt, and chuck steak are all good and economical. Variety meats lend themselves to slow cooking. Oxtail provides a rich stew and ox kidney and liver, which tend to be strongly flavored, are often cooked with stewing beef or bacon.

Stews have the great merit of being suitable for cooking in advance, for reheating or freezing. Many casseroles improve with reheating because their sauce continues its work of tenderizing even as it cools.

Beef Burgundy

½ cup oil
2 lbs. top round, cut into 1-inch cubes
1 carrot, thinly sliced
1 large onion, thinly sliced
¼ cup flour
2 cups dry red wine
salt and pepper
2 cloves garlic, peeled and crushed
bouquet garni
1 cup pearl onions, peeled
1 tablespoon sugar
¼ cup butter
¼ lb. lean bacon, cut in strips
1 cup mushrooms, chopped

1 Heat three-quarters of the oil in a heavy stewpan, put the pieces of beef into it and brown over high heat. Remove the meat, then pour out any remaining oil and add the slices of carrot and onion. Let them brown lightly, then add the flour and cook it, stirring constantly with a wooden spoon.

2 Mix in all the wine. Bring it to a boil and allow at least a third of it to evaporate on high heat. Return the meat to the pan and add enough cold water to cover it. Add salt, pepper, the garlic and the bouquet garni. Cover and cook gently for 2½ hours.

3 Put the pearl onions in a pan with the sugar, the butter and enough water to cover. Cover and cook until the water has evaporated. When a golden caramel mixture remains, roll the small onions in it and place to one side.

4 Heat the rest of the oil in a pan and lightly fry the bacon. Drain and reserve. Fry the mushrooms in the same oil and reserve.

5 When the stew is cooked, strain the sauce, then return it to the pan. Add the pearl onions, bacon and mushrooms and cook for a further 10 minutes.

Serves 6

Czardaz Beef with Caraway Rice

2 tablespoons oil
2 lbs. stewing beef, cut into 1-inch cubes
3 branches celery, chopped
1 large onion, sliced
⅔ cup water
½ beef bouillon cube
1 lb. canned pineapple chunks, with juice
1 tablespoon chopped parsley
pinch sugar
1 tablespoon tomato paste
few drops Worcestershire sauce
salt and pepper
1½ cups long grain rice
2 tablespoons butter
2 teaspoons caraway seeds

1 Preheat the oven to 350°F.

2 Heat the oil in a skillet. Brown the meat in it, remove and place in a casserole. Add the celery and the onion to the oil and sauté for 3 minutes, then add to the casserole.

3 Pour the water into a pan, bring to a boil and crumble in the bouillon cube. Drain the pineapple and add the juice to the stock with the parsley, sugar, tomato paste, Worcestershire sauce and salt and pepper to taste. Pour over the meat in the casserole, cover, and cook for 1½ hours, adding more stock if necessary.

4 15 minutes before the end of cooking, add the pineapple.

5 To cook the rice, first place it in a strainer and wash it thoroughly under cold running water. Remove any discolored grains. Place it in a large pan of boiling, slightly salted water. Boil for 12 minutes or until the rice is tender. Turn off heat and steam covered for 10 minutes. Gently stir in the butter and the caraway seeds.

Serves 6

Czardaz Beef with Caraway Rice is a fruity casserole with a Russian flavor which will delight your family and friends

Austrian Beef Casserole with Horseradish Sauce

2 lbs. stewing beef
¼ cup oil
6 small onions
6⅓ cups water
3 beef bouillon cubes
bouquet garni
6 leeks

For the Horseradish Sauce:
⅔ cup water
2 tablespoons white vinegar
⅔ cup horseradish, scraped
⅔ cup cooking apple, peeled and cored
½ cup fresh white breadcrumbs
¼ cup light cream

1 Cut the meat into 1½-inch cubes.

2 Heat the oil in a heavy pan and brown the meat, covered with a lid, for 8 minutes. Stir often.

3 Slice the onions and add to the meat, and brown for 3 minutes.

4 Cover with the water mixed with the beef cubes and bouquet garni.

5 Wash the leeks, split into four, tie in a bundle and put with the meat.

6 Bring to a boil, and remove the scum as it rises, with a spoon. Simmer for 2-2½ hours until the meat is tender.

7 Meanwhile, put the water and vinegar in a bowl and grate the horseradish and apple into it. Soak for 1 hour. Drain the liquid off, and mix the breadcrumbs and cream into the mixture. Place in a bowl.

8 When the meat is cooked, the broth may be strained off and served separately as soup. Remove the leeks, discard the string, and place on top of the meat.

Serves 6

Beef Niçoise is a casserole from the Mediterranean, cooked in wine and garnished with tomatoes and black olives

Tip: In Central Europe the broth would be served with liver dumplings.

Beef Niçoise

2 lbs. stewing beef
¼ lb. lean bacon
¼ cup oil
4 onions, sliced
2 cloves garlic, peeled and crushed
bouquet garni
¼ cup flour
1¼ cups wine
1¼ cups water
1 beef bouillon cube
2 tablespoons tomato paste
6 tomatoes, skinned, seeded and chopped
salt and pepper
1 tablespoon chopped parsley
6 black olives

1 Cut the meat into 1-inch cubes and the bacon into strips.

2 Heat the oil in a thick pan. Brown the beef and bacon for 8 minutes, covered with a lid. Stir often.

3 Add the onion, garlic and bouquet garni, cook for 4 minutes. Sprinkle on the flour, cook for 1 minute.

4 Add the wine, water, bouillon cube, tomato paste and chopped tomatoes. Season. Bring to a boil and simmer for 1½-2 hours until the meat is tender. Or cook in the oven with a lid on at 350°F. for the same time.

5 When ready to serve, add the chopped parsley and olives.

Serves 6

Austrian Beef Casserole with Horseradish Sauce is a tasty way of serving beef, with leeks and a creamy sauce

Look 'n Cook Daube of Beef with Red Wine

1 The ingredients 2 Cut the lean salt pork and white salt pork fat into strips. Put the pork fat in a dish, sprinkle with brandy and chopped parsley and chill 3 Cut the meat into cubes, and thread each piece with a strip of fat 4 Place the ingredients in a bowl, and add the mushrooms 5 Pour on the red wine, oil and brandy. Season and marinate for 2 hours. Remove the meat and salt pork and dry. Put some oil in the casserole and

brown the meat **6** Add the vegetables and brown. Add the marinade and water **7** Bring to a boil and cook in the oven for 2½ hours at 350°F. **8** When the meat is tender, remove the fat with a ladle, and remove the bouquet gar-ni and pork rind **9** Place the meat on a serving dish and pour the sauce over. Sprinkle with the parsley and serve with new potatoes.

Daube of Beef with Red Wine

½ lb. lean salt pork
½ lb. salt pork fat (optional)
¼ cup brandy or port
1 tablespoon chopped parsley
4 lbs. top round of beef
3 large carrots, chopped
3 large onions, chopped
3 large tomatoes, chopped
3 cloves garlic, crushed
8 mushrooms
½ bottle red wine
½ cup oil
salt
12 peppercorns, crushed
pinch mixed spice
1¼ cups water
bouquet garni
2 tablespoons flour
   (optional)

1 Cut the lean salt pork into strips, and scald by plunging in boiling water for 1 minute. Cool.

2 Cut the pork fat (if used) into strips 2 x ¼ inches, sprinkle with a few drops of brandy and a pinch of parsley. Chill for ½ hour.

3 Cut the meat into 1½-inch cubes. If using the pork fat, take a larding needle, and thread each piece with a strip of fat.

4 Place the salt pork and the meat in a bowl with the carrots, onions and tomatoes, garlic, and mushrooms.

5 Pour on the wine, brandy and half of the oil. Add salt, the peppercorns and the mixed spice and marinate for 2 hours. Remove the meat and dry on absorbent paper.

6 Preheat the oven to 350°F.

7 Put the remainder of the oil in a thick pan, add the meat and salt pork and brown for 5 minutes. Add the vegetables and brown for 3 minutes. Add the marinade, water, and bouquet garni and bring to a boil. Put in the oven with a lid on

and cook for 2½ hours, or until the meat is tender.

8 When cooked, remove the fat from the surface carefully with a ladle. Remove the bouquet garni.

9 If you wish, thicken the daube with the flour mixed with ½ cup water and cook for 2 minutes, stirring gently.

10 Place the meat on a serving dish, pour on the sauce and sprinkle with the remainder of the chopped parsley. Serve with new potatoes.

Serves 8

Steak Romanov

1 lb. Filet Mignon
¼ cup oil
1 medium onion, or 3 shallots, chopped
1 tablespoon paprika
2 tablespoons tomato paste
⅔ cup water
⅔ cup whipping cream
1 tablespoon vodka
salt and pepper

1 Remove the skin and fat from the meat and cut into cubes ¾ inch thick.

2 Heat the oil in a skillet. Brown the meat for 4 minutes, stirring constantly. Remove from the pan.

3 In the same pan, fry the onions gently for 2 minutes without coloring.

4 Sprinkle on the paprika and add the tomato paste and cook for 2 minutes, stirring.

5 Add the water and boil for 5 minutes. Beat the cream until stiff, add to the pan and boil for 2 minutes.

6 Reheat the meat in the sauce for 3 minutes. Remove from the heat.

7 Just before serving, add the vodka and check the seasoning. Serve with boiled rice.

Serves 4

Variation

This recipe for Steak Romanov is given as an illustration of a style of cooking steak in a skillet in front of guests. Because it is cooked in only a few minutes, tenderloin must be used so that the meat is both cooked and tender.

The Russians tend to use sour cream, rather than the fresh cream we have used, and they call it Sauce Smitane. If you wish to try this, you can buy sour cream, or make your own by adding a few drops of lemon juice to the fresh cream.

To make Sauce Smitane, gently sauté some chopped onions in butter. Add wine and reduce. Pour in the sour cream and boil for a few moments. Strain through a sieve and add lemon juice. Try this sauce with beef, or with chicken, veal or lamb.

Another Russan variation on Steak Romanov would be to use caraway seeds instead of paprika, and to add a little kummel, which is a liqueur flavored with caraway seeds.

The classic dish of Beef Strogonoff is another variation of a dish to be cooked in public. For this the tenderloin is cut into thin strips and cooked with mushrooms and sour cream. The dish was created by the head chef of the Count Strogonoff in the 1880s in Russia. The dish was almost unknown in Europe, until the great mass of Russian emigrants came to France after the Russian Revolution. The dish then became very popular in the big hotels of the French Riviera in the 1920s and gradually spread through Europe as the head waiters of famous restaurants enjoyed the drama of preparing this dish, flaming in brandy, before honored customers. Brandy is the traditional spirit used, although other spirits may be added.

Look 'n Cook Steak Romanov

1 Cut the tenderloin into cubes 2 Heat the oil in a skillet and brown the meat, stirring constantly 3 Remove the meat from the pan 4 Fry the chopped onions gently, sprinkle on the paprika and add the tomato paste and stir. Cook for 2 minutes. Add the water 5 Add the cream, stir and boil 6 Reheat the meat in the sauce. Remove from the heat, add the vodka and season

Country Beef and Olive Casserole

1½ lbs. stewing beef
2 tablespoons oil
3 carrots, sliced
2 small onions, quartered
1 branch celery, sliced
1 clove garlic, peeled and crushed
¼ cup flour
1¼ cups water
⅔ cup sherry
1 lb. canned tomatoes
1 beef bouillon cube
1 bay leaf
few sprigs parsley
salt and pepper
6 stuffed green olives, sliced

1 Cut the beef into 1½-inch cubes.

2 Preheat the oven to 350°F.

3 Heat the oil in a saucepan and fry the meat until browned. Remove from the pan.

4 Add the carrots, onions, celery and garlic to the pan. Sauté over low heat for 5 minutes.

5 Stir in the flour and cook gently for a few minutes, then add the water, sherry and canned tomatoes. Crumble in the bouillon cube and stir well. Add the bay leaf and parsley and season with salt and pepper.

6 Bring to a boil, stirring all the time until it thickens. Transfer to an ovenproof dish, cover with a lid and cook in the oven for 2½ hours. Remove the bay leaf and parsley. Stir in the olives and serve with green beans and boiled potatoes.

Serves 4

Country Beef and Olive Casserole has a distinctive Spanish flavor with its tomatoes and stuffed olives

Sweet and Sour Beef

4 beef sausages
2 tablespoons oil
1 onion, chopped
½ lb. diced, boiled beef

For the Sauce:
1¼ cups water
½ cucumber, cut into chunks
2 branches celery, sliced
1 carrot, cut into thin strips
¼ cup soy sauce
1 beef bouillon cube
1 clove garlic, peeled and chopped
1 tablespoon fresh gingerroot, peeled and chopped
1½ tablespoons honey
2 tablespoons vinegar
1½ tablespoons cornstarch
salt and pepper

1 Broil or fry the sausages. Cool and cut in thick slices.

2 Heat the oil and fry the onion until soft, then add the beef and sausages. Fry for 5 minutes.

3 Bring the water to a boil, and cook the cucumber, celery and carrot for 5 minutes so that they are still crisp.

4 Add the soy sauce and crumble in the bouillon cube. Add the garlic, ginger, honey and vinegar and stir well. Mix the cornstarch with a little water and stir into the sauce. Boil for 3 minutes until it thickens, stirring all the time. Stir in the sausage, beef and onion mixture and simmer for 10 minutes.

5 Arrange on a serving dish, surrounded by boiled rice.

Serves 4

Tip: For a sweeter and more colorful sauce, try adding strips of sweet red pepper, pineapple chunks and tangerine sections to the sauce before serving.

Sweet and Sour Beef, Curried Meat Balls and Beef Farmhouse Pie are three supper dishes for cold evenings

1 The ingredients 2 Peel the onions and slice them finely 3 Cut the meat into 1-inch cubes 4 Sauté the onion in the oil for 4 minutes until pale brown 5 Add the cubed meat, reduce the heat and cook gently for 8 minutes, stirring from time to time 6 While the meat is cooking, remove the seeds from the pepper and cut the flesh into shreds. Skin, seed and chop the tomatoes 7 Add the paprika, cumin, garlic, seasoning and mar-

joram to the pan and cook for 1 minute **8** Add the
tomatoes and pepper and cook for another 10 minutes
9 Stir in the wine and water and crumble in the beef
bouillon cubes. Cook gently for 1½ hours **10** Boil the
potatoes **11** Thicken the goulash and add the lemon
juice to the cream **12** Serve the goulash with the sour
cream and the potatoes

Beef Goulash

⅓ cup oil
3 medium onions, thinly sliced
1½ lbs. stewing beef (chuck steak) cut in 1-inch cubes
1 tablespoon paprika
pinch cumin
2 cloves garlic, crushed
salt and pepper
pinch marjoram
3 tomatoes, skinned, seeded and chopped
1 green pepper, shredded
⅔ cup red wine
4¼ cups water
2 beef bouillon cubes
4 medium-size potatoes, peeled
3 tablespoons flour
juice half lemon
⅔ cup light cream

1 Heat the oil in a pan and sauté the onion for 4 minutes until pale brown. Add the meat, reduce the heat and cook gently for 8 minutes, stirring from time to time.

2 Add the paprika, cumin, garlic, seasoning and marjoram and cook for 1 minute more. Add the tomatoes and pepper and simmer for another 10 minutes. Stir in the wine and water and crumble in the bouillon cubes. Cook gently for 1½ hours.

3 Toward the end of the cooking time, boil the potatoes in salted water for 18 minutes.

4 When ready to serve, dissolve the flour in ⅔ cup water, stir into the meat and cook for 2-3 minutes until thickened.

5 Add the lemon juice to the cream. Serve the goulash with the sour cream and the boiled potatoes.

Serves 6

Tip: Shell pasta or rice can be served with this dish in place of the boiled potatoes, if preferred.

Beef Casseroles

Hungarian Meatballs Casserole

1 lb. ground beef
½ cup breadcrumbs
1 egg
salt and pepper
1 tablespoon chopped parsley
½ cup flour
¼ cup oil
3 large onions, sliced
2 tablespoons paprika
¼ cup tomato paste
2 tablespoons flour
1 bouillon cube
1¼ cups boiling water
pinch caraway seeds (optional)
3 medium-size potatoes, sliced

1 Mix the ground meat, breadcrumbs, egg, salt and pepper, and parsley in a bowl. Make 12 meatballs and dust with the flour.

2 Preheat the oven to 375°F.

3 Heat most of the oil in a skillet, brown the meatballs and place in a casserole.

4 To make the sauce, slice the onions, and brown in the rest of the oil. Add the paprika and tomato paste and cook for 2 minutes. Sprinkle on the flour. Stir; cook for 1 minute.

5 Add the bouillon cube mixed with the boiling water. Season and add the caraway seeds.

6 Pour the sauce over the meatballs. Arrange slices of potato around the dish and bake for 45 minutes.

Serves 4

Hellenic Casserole

1 lb. eggplant, peeled, sliced
¼ cup oil
2 large onions, thinly sliced
1 clove garlic, crushed
1 lb. ground beef
2 tablespoons tomato paste
salt and pepper
1¼ cups boiling water
1 beef bouillon cube
3 medium-size tomatoes, sliced
3 medium-size potatoes, sliced
2 eggs
⅔ cup light cream
½ cup grated cheese
3 tablespoons grated Parmesan cheese

1 Sprinkle the eggplant with salt and leave for ½ hour. Wash off the bitter juices and dry.

2 Heat the oil in a skillet and cook the eggplant slices for ½ minute on each side. Remove from the pan.

3 Preheat the oven to 350°F.

4 Fry the onions and garlic until golden-brown. Add the ground meat and brown, stirring. Add the tomato paste and cook for 2 minutes. Season. Add the boiling water mixed with the bouillon cube. Simmer for 10 minutes.

5 Arrange the eggplant, meat and onions, sliced tomatoes and sliced potatoes, in layers in a casserole and bake for 35 minutes.

6 Beat the eggs with the cream and stir in the cheese. Pour on the casserole and return to the oven for 20 minutes until the topping is golden-brown.

Serves 4

The center of our table shows, from top to bottom: Hungarian Meatballs Casserole, Steak and Kidney Pudding, Hellenic Casserole

Look 'n Cook Steak and Kidney Pudding

10

11

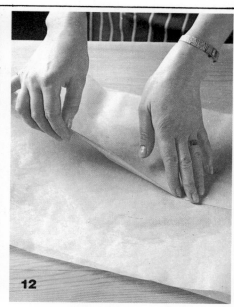

12

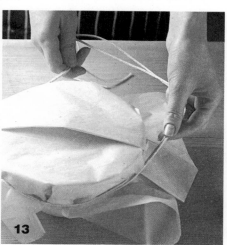

13

14

15

1 Sift the flour into a bowl and add the suet **2** Pour on enough water to form a dough **3** Roll out into a circle, reserving ¼ dough for the lid **4** Grease a pudding dish and line it with the dough **5** The onion, kidney and steak, chopped **6** Place the slices of kidney on the strips of beef **7** Roll them up and dip them in the seasoned flour **8** Pour on the stock **9** and **10** Roll out the pastry for the lid. Seal the edges well **11** Grease a large sheet of parchment paper **12** and **13** Make a pleat in the paper, then tie it around the basin **14** and **15** After 3½ hours' steaming either invert the pudding onto a serving dish or spoon it from the pudding dish

Old English Steak and Kidney Pudding

2¼ cups self-rising flour
pinch salt
¼ lb. beef suet, shredded

For the Filling:
1 large onion
6 ozs. beef kidney
1 lb. best stewing steak (rump, bottom round)
¼ cup flour, lightly salted
3 tablespoons beef stock

1 To make the pastry, sift the flour into a mixing bowl with the salt. Mix in the suet. Add enough cold water to form a dough.

2 Roll out on a floured board in a circle 10 inches in diameter. Cut away ¼ of the circle and set aside for the lid.

3 Grease a 1¾ quart pudding dish and line it with the dough, allowing a small overlap around the top. Let rest in a cool place.

4 Chop the onion finely. Remove skin and core from the kidney and slice it. Cut the steak into strips about 5 inches long. Place a slice of kidney on each and roll up. Dip the rolls in seasoned flour and place them in layers in the pudding dish, alternating with layers of sliced onion, until the dish is filled. Pour on the stock.

5 Roll out the dough reserved for the lid. Dampen the edges of the pastry, put on the lid and press the edges well together. Grease a large sheet of parchment paper and make a pleat in the middle to allow the pudding room to rise. Tie the paper onto the pudding dish with kitchen string and steam in a double boiler. Serve hot.

Serves 6

Tips: To save time, this Steak and Kidney Pudding can be cooked in a pressure cooker. First cook the steak, kidney and onion mixture in the stock for 15 minutes at high pressure. Then make the pastry. Line and fill the pudding dish as described in the recipe. Then follow your manufacturer's instructions for length of cooking at pressure.

Oxtail Matilda

2½ cups black tea
1⅓ cups prunes
2 lbs. oxtail, cut up
6 tablespoons flour
2 onions, sliced
2 branches celery, sliced
2 carrots, sliced
2½ cups water
2 beef bouillon cubes
¼ cup tomato paste
bouquet garni
2 cloves garlic, peeled and crushed
1 tablespoon sugar
salt and pepper
6 baby carrots, trimmed
12 pearl onions, peeled

1 Pour the tea into a pan and soak the prunes in it for 3 hours. Then bring to a boil and simmer for 15 minutes.

2 Preheat the oven to 350°F.

3 Wash the oxtail in cold water and dry. Trim off excess fat and roll in the flour. Place in a skillet over very gentle heat for 25 minutes, until the oxtail becomes brown and the fat melts. Remove and place in a casserole. Lightly sauté the sliced onions, celery and carrots in the fat, then add to the oxtail. Bring the water to a boil, crumble in the bouillon cubes, and pour onto the oxtail. Add the tomato paste, bouquet garni, garlic and 1 teaspoon sugar. Season to taste. Cover, and place in the oven to cook for 3 hours.

4 When the oxtail is tender, take it out of the casserole and keep hot. Strain the sauce, discard any floating fat and add the prune liquor. Replace the meat, and heat.

5 Place the baby carrots in a pan with enough water to cover. Add the butter and remaining sugar, bring to a boil and simmer for 4 minutes. Add the small onions and cook for a further 8 minutes. Serve hot, surrounded by the prunes, onions and carrots.

Serves 6

Winter Stew

1½ lbs. stewing beef
6 ozs. beef kidney
¼ cup flour
2 tablespoons meat drippings
1 large onion, sliced
2 large carrots, sliced
2 small turnips, sliced
2 cups cider
pinch ground ginger
bouquet garni
salt and pepper

For the Savory Dumplings:
1 cup + 2 tablespoons self-rising flour
pinch salt
¼ cup sausage meat
½ cup shredded beef suet
pinch mixed herbs
⅔ cup cider

1 Cut the beef into 1-inch cubes. Skin, core and slice the kidneys. Dredge in the seasoned flour. Heat the drippings in a skillet and fry the meat until lightly brown. Add the onion and fry for 3 minutes more. Transfer to a heavy-bottomed pan. Fry the carrot and turnip for 2 minutes, then transfer to the pan. Pour on the cider, add the ginger, bouquet garni, and season to taste. Cover and simmer for 1½ hours.

Oxtail Casserole is a hearty stew of oxtail and vegetables

2 To make the dumplings, sift the flour and salt into a bowl and mix in the sausage meat. Add the suet and herbs and mix to a soft dough with the cider. Divide into 12 balls and roll in flour.

3 Remove the meat with a slotted spoon and pass the sauce through a strainer. Replace the meat, add the dumplings, and simmer for a further ½ hour.

4 Place the remaining carrot and turnip in a pan of boiling, salted water. Simmer for 15 minutes, drain and add to the stew.

Serves 6

Stewed Oxtail

2 lbs. oxtail, jointed
2 tablespoons meat drippings
1 onion, sliced
2 carrots, sliced
2 turnips, sliced
2 branches celery, sliced
6 tablespoons flour
2 tablespoons tomato paste
bouquet garni
4¼ cups beef stock
salt and pepper
1 tablespoon chopped parsley

1 Preheat the oven to 350°F.

2 Remove excess fat from the ox-
tail. Heat the drippings in a pan and brown the oxtail. Add the onion, 1 carrot, 1 turnip and the celery. Fry them lightly. Pour off surplus fat, sprinkle on the flour and transfer to a casserole. Stir in the tomato paste and the bouquet garni. Pour on the stock and season to taste. Bring to a boil, skim and cover. Cook in the oven for 3 hours.

3 Simmer the remaining sliced carrot and turnip in a little water for 5 minutes. When the oxtail is tender, strain the sauce. Check the seasoning, add the carrot and turnip, bring to a boil and pour over the meat. Serve sprinkled with the chopped parsley.

Serves 6

Quick Chicken and Beef Casserole

1¼ cups white sauce
¼ cup dry sherry
salt and pepper
⅔ cup cooked beef, cut into strips
1 small dill pickle, sliced
⅔ cup cooked chicken, diced
⅔ cup sliced mushrooms
⅔ cup ham, cut into strips
½ cup almond halves

1 Heat the white sauce and stir in the sherry and season with salt and pepper.

2 Preheat the oven to 350°F.

3 Place the beef and dill pickle in the bottom of an ovenproof dish. Pour in half of the white sauce. Put a layer of chicken, mushrooms and ½ cup of the ham on top. Pour on the remaining white sauce and sprinkle with the almonds and ham strips.

4 Place in the oven and warm through for 15 minutes.

Serves 4

Tip: This casserole is especially quick to make and all sorts of left-over meat could be used such as pork or turkey or even veal. For extra body, mix in some canned butter beans.

Mexican Hotpot

2 tablespoons oil
1 large onion, chopped
1 green pepper, seeded and chopped
1 sweet red pepper, seeded and chopped
1 lb. ground beef
pinch paprika
pinch chili powder
¼ cup flour
2 tablespoons tomato paste
1¾ cups water
1 beef bouillon cube
bouquet garni
salt and pepper
1 cup canned kidney beans, drained

1 Heat the oil in a saucepan and fry the onion until soft. Add the green and red peppers and cook for 1 minute. Add the ground beef and brown for 5 minutes, stirring occasionally.

2 Stir in the paprika, chili powder and flour and cook for 2 minutes. Add the tomato paste and water, and crumble in the bouillon cube. Bring to a boil, stirring all the time, then add the bouquet garni, lower the heat and cook gently on top of the stove for 30 minutes.

3 Season with salt and pepper to taste and add the drained kidney beans. Continue cooking for another 5 minutes until the kidney beans are heated through, then serve with plain boiled rice.

Serves 4

Tip: If you like really hot spicy food, try increasing the amount of chili powder and adding some corn for a more authentic South American flavor.

Beef Cobbler

¼ cup oil
1½ lbs. stewing beef, cubed
1 onion, chopped
1 carrot, chopped
¼ cup flour
2 tablespoons tomato paste
1¼ cups water
1¼ cups beer
1 beef bouillon cube
1 clove garlic, peeled and crushed
pinch rosemary
salt and pepper
1 tablespoon milk
1 tablespoon chopped parsley

For the Cobbler Topping:
1½ cups self-rising flour
pinch salt
2 branches celery, finely minced
2 tablespoons chopped parsley
3 tablespoons butter
½ cup milk

1 Heat the oil in a pan and brown the stewing beef for 5 minutes. Add the onion and carrot and cook for 2-3 more minutes until soft. Stir in the flour and cook for a further minute.

2 Preheat the oven to 350°F.

3 Add the tomato paste, water and beer and crumble in the bouillon cube. Add the garlic and rosemary and bring to a boil.

4 Transfer to an overproof casserole dish and place in the oven for 1½ hours.

5 Meanwhile, make the cobbler topping. Mix together the flour, salt, celery and parsley in a bowl. Rub in the butter until the mixture resembles fine breadcrumbs. Add the milk, a little at a time, and mix well to make a soft dough.

6 Knead the dough lightly on a floured surface and roll out ¾ inch thick. Using a 3-inch cutter, cut out as many circles as you can. Then, using a ½-inch cutter, cut a hole in the center of each dough circle.

7 Increase the oven temperature to 425°F. Remove the casserole and season to taste. Arrange the dough rings, overlapping each other, around the top and brush with milk.

8 Bake for a further 20 minutes until the topping is golden-brown. Garnish with chopped parsley.

Serves 4

Mexican Hotpot, Beef Cobbler and Quick Chicken and Beef Casserole are all deliciously different ideas for casseroling beef

10

11

12

13

1 Slice the onion into thin rings **2** Skin and slice the tomatoes **3** Slice the liver **4** Season the liver with salt and pepper and flour **5** Arrange the floured liver in layers with the onion rings in a casserole **6** Lay the slices of lean bacon on top and repeat the layers **7** Lay the sliced tomatoes on the top, sprinkled with oregano. Mix the tomato paste with the stock **8** Pour the stock into the casserole **9** Mix the flour and water to make a firm paste **10** Put this paste around the edge of the casserole **11** Put on the lid and press firmly to make an airtight seal and cook in the oven for 1½ hours **12** Chip away the paste **13** The finished dish

Liver and Bacon Casserole

1 large onion
3 large tomatoes
1 lb. beef liver
salt and pepper
2¼ cups flour
8 slices lean bacon
1 teaspoon dried oregano
1 bouillon cube
1 cup water
¼ cup tomato paste

1 Slice the onion, tomatoes and liver. Season the liver and dip in ½ cup of the flour.

2 Arrange half of the floured liver in the casserole, with half of the onion on top. Lay half of the bacon above and repeat the layers of liver, onion and bacon. Lay the sliced tomatoes on top and sprinkle with oregano.

3 Preheat the oven to 350°F.

4 Mix the bouillon cube with ⅔ cup of the water. Stir in the tomato paste and pour into the casserole.

5 Make a firm paste from the rest of the flour and the water and press around the edge of the casserole.

6 Put the lid on and press firmly to make an airtight seal.

7 Cook in the oven for 1½ hours.

8 Carefully chip away the cooked paste, and serve.

Serves 4

Ground Beef Casserole is easy and economical to make on cold winter days and is a tasty lunch for the family

Ground Beef Casserole

1¼ cups chopped onions
¼ cup drippings or fat
1 lb. lean ground beef
2 tablespoons tomato paste
⅔ cup beer
1¼ cups water
1 bouillon cube
1 tablespoon sugar
pinch mace
1½ tablespoons cornstarch
⅔ cup water
salt and pepper
4 medium-size potatoes
1 egg yolk
3 tablespoons butter
salt and pepper
6 mushrooms

1 Gently fry the chopped onions in

the fat until brown. Add the ground beef and cook, stirring, until brown.

2 Add the tomato paste, beer, water, bouillon cube, sugar and mace, and simmer for 35 minutes.

3 Meanwhile, peel the potatoes and boil. Mash and mix with the egg yolk and 2 tablespoons of the butter and season.

4 Add the cornstarch mixed with water to the meat to thicken. Season with salt.

5 Spread a thin layer of the hot mashed potato over the meat. Brown under the broiler.

6 Place the remainder of the mashed potato in a decorator's bag with a ½-inch star tube and pipe a crisscross pattern, and decorate with halved mushrooms, lightly sautéed in ½ oz. of butter.

Serves 4

Sausages in Mexican Tomato Sauce

1 lb. link sausages
3 branches celery, sliced
½ cup salted peanuts

For the Mexican Tomato Sauce:
1 tablespoon butter
2 onions, finely chopped
2 carrots, finely chopped
1 branch celery, finely chopped
2 tablespoons flour
2 tablespoons tomato paste
½ cup chopped sweet red pepper
1 chicken bouillon cube
1¼ cups boiling water
1 clove garlic, crushed
½ bay leaf
sprig thyme
salt and pepper
3 tablespoons medium sherry

Sausages in Mexican Tomato Sauce is an original way of serving sausages with peanuts and celery

1 To make the sauce, put the butter in a saucepan, add the finely chopped onions, carrots and celery and brown slightly.

2 Add the flour. Stir and brown slightly, until the flour looks sandy.

3 Add the tomato paste and chopped red pepper. Stir well. Cool slightly.

4 Add the bouillon cube mixed with the boiling water, add the garlic and herbs, season and simmer for 1 hour, then check the seasoning.

5 Strain the sauce and stir in the sherry.

6 Meanwhile, broil the sausages and keep them hot in a dish.

7 Cook the celery for 5 minutes in boiling water. Drain and add to the sausages.

8 Pour on the sauce, and keep hot.

9 When ready to serve, garnish with salted peanuts. Serve with creamed potatoes, browned under the broiler and garnished with sliced tomatoes.

Serves 4

Variation: This Tomato Sauce may also be used with leftover cold meat. Arrange the meat in individual dishes, with some green beans. Make the sauce as shown, but omit the red pepper and sherry. Add blanched strips of orange peel and the juice of an orange to the sauce. Pour on and reheat for at least 15 minutes in the oven and serve garnished with hard-boiled eggs.

Beef Hotpots

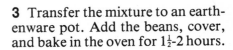

Hotpot Parisienne

3 cups cooked lima beans
1½ lbs. stewing beef, cut into
  1-inch cubes
¼ cup oil
2 onions, chopped
1 clove garlic, crushed
2 tablespoons flour
1 tablespoon tomato paste
1¼ cups water
⅔ cup white wine
bouquet garni

sprig rosemary
salt and pepper
2 zucchini, sliced
4 tomatoes, quartered

1 If using dried beans, soak them overnight in water, then bring to a boil and simmer until tender. Rinse and drain.

2 Preheat oven to 350°F. Brown the meat in the oil for 5 minutes in a saucepan. Add the onion and garlic and cook for 2 minutes. Sprinkle in the flour and cook for 2 minutes to brown it. Stir in the tomato paste and then pour in the water and wine. Season with the bouquet garni, rosemary, salt and pepper. Bring it to a boil and simmer for 10 minutes.

Hotpot Parisienne makes a colorful and economical dish for a dinner party — serve with boiled or savory rice

3 Transfer the mixture to an earthenware pot. Add the beans, cover, and bake in the oven for 1½-2 hours.

4 Remove the hotpot from the oven, add the zucchini and tomatoes, and return to the oven for 15 minutes. Check seasoning, and serve hot.

Serves 6

Beef in Cider Hotpot

3 tablespoons butter
1½ lbs. top round, cut into thin
  slices
1 large onion, sliced
2 large carrots, peeled and sliced
2 turnips, peeled and diced
6 tablespoons flour
1¾ cups cider, or 1¼ cups apple juice
  with ⅔ cup water and 1 tablespoon
  vinegar
salt and pepper
1 beef bouillon cube, crumbled
3 medium-size potatoes, peeled
  and thinly sliced
¾ cup grated cheese

1 Preheat oven to 350°F. Melt the butter and fry the beef slices for 5 minutes. Remove. Add the onion, carrots and turnips to the pan and sauté gently for 10 minutes. Stir in the flour for 1 minute. Remove from heat and pour in the cider or apple juice. Bring to a boil, then add seasoning and the bouillon cube. Cook for 5 minutes.

2 Pour into an earthenware pot and arrange the potato slices on top. Cover and cook in the oven for 1½-2 hours. Increase the oven temperature to 400°F. Sprinkle the grated cheese on top and bake for 15-20 minutes uncovered until the cheese is golden-brown. Serve.

Serves 4

Beef in Cider Hotpot is a delicious variation on the traditional hotpot — the beef is cooked in cider and topped with cheese

Beef Fondues

Sukiyaki

1 cup rice
salt
3 cups finely shredded green cabbage
1 large leek, cleaned and sliced diagonally
8 ozs. canned water chestnuts
2 large carrots, thinly sliced
5 radishes, sliced
4 unbroken egg yolks

1 lb. tenderloin, cut in ⅛-inch slices about 2 inches long

For the Stock:
2½ cups water
2 beef bouillon cubes
¼ cup soy sauce
⅔ cup dry sherry

1 Boil the rice in salted water until just tender. Rinse and drain. Prepare the vegetables and arrange in a wide dish.

2 At the table, serve each diner with a bowl of rice and a side dish containing an unbroken egg yolk. Bring the water to a boil in the fondue pot. Crumble in the bouillon cubes and stir to dissolve. Pour in the soy sauce and sherry,

---

Sukiyaki is a traditional Japanese dish — the guests cook their own meat and help themselves to dips and vegetables

bring back to a boil and keep just under boiling point.

3 Place pieces of each vegetable in the stock, and a piece of meat for each diner in the middle. Diners may remove the meat when it is cooked to their individual taste — a couple of minutes should be enough. Serve the vegetables, also cooked to taste, on the rice, and dip the pieces of meat in the egg yolk before eating. Replenish the stock with vegetables and meat as required.

Serves 4

Beef Fondue with Dips

1¼ cups mayonnaise
1 teaspoon curry powder or 1 tablespoon curry sauce
1 clove garlic, crushed
1 tablespoon chopped fresh parsley and chives
3 cups water
2 beef bouillon cubes
⅔ cup dry sherry
bouquet garni
2 fresh mint leaves
salt and pepper
1 lb. tenderloin, diced

1 Divide the mayonnaise between 2 dishes. Into one, mix the curry powder or sauce to make a curry dip. Into the other stir the garlic, parsley and chives to make a garlic herb dip.

2 At the table, boil the water, add the bouillon cubes, sherry, bouquet garni, mint leaves, and season to taste. Keep just below boiling point. Diners take a piece of meat on a fondue fork and leave it in the stock 2-5 minutes until cooked to taste. Dip the meat into one of the dips before eating.

Serves 4

Tip: Other fondue sauces include horseradish, tomato, mustard or tartar.

Beef Fondue with Dips is fun to eat — diners boil meat at the table and flavor it with dips and sauces

Economy Beef

Texturized soy protein (or textured vegetable protein) has proved of great help to cooks to stretch meat further and thus economize, especially with beef. It reduces the need for starchy additives like potato and has the same nutritional value as meat. Its neutral taste absorbs the flavor of whatever it is cooked with. To increase its flavor, fry at the same time as the beef.

Curried Beef and Golden Rice

1 cup long grain rice
pinch turmeric
½ lb. ground beef
1 carrot, diced
1 tablespoon curry powder
1 teaspoon shredded coconut
2 tablespoons raisins
1 apple, peeled, cored and diced

1 Boil the rice in plenty of salted water to which a good pinch of turmeric has been added. Simmer until tender, rinse and drain. Keep warm.

2 Make the basic ground beef, according to the recipe, but add the diced carrot to the onion before frying, and stir in the curry powder when browning the meat. Stir in the coconut, raisins and apple after adding the soy protein.

3 Arrange the rice around the edge of a large dish, and pour the curry into the middle. Serve hot.

Serves 4

Basic Ground Beef

1 large onion, chopped
2 tablespoons oil
1 lb. ground beef
¼ cup flour
2 tablespoons tomato paste
1¼ cups water
1 beef bouillon cube
salt, pepper, pinch mace
½ cup reconstituted texturized soy protein

1 Fry the onion gently in the oil until soft. Stir in the beef and flour and cook until browned. Add the tomato paste and continue to cook for 2 minutes.

2 Pour in the water, in which the bouillon cube has been dissolved, and season with salt, pepper and a pinch of mace. Add the soy protein. Simmer for ½ hour, stirring from time to time.

Serves 4

Beef and Vegetable Vol-au-vent

one 6-inch pastry shell
½ lb. ground beef
½ cup frozen peas
2 zucchini, peeled and sliced

1 Preheat the oven to 425°F. Bake the pastry shell for 20-25 minutes or until golden-brown. Keep warm.

2 Meanwhile, prepare the basic ground beef, according to the recipe. While it is cooking, add the peas to boiling, salted water. Bring back to a boil, add the zucchini and cook them together for 4 minutes.

3 When the beef is cooked, stir in the peas and zucchini and pour the mixture into the pastry case. Serve immediately.

Serves 4

Stuffed Crêpes

½ lb. ground beef
½ green pepper, diced
1 cup corn kernels
1 teaspoon chili powder
1¼ cups crêpe batter
1 cup grated cheese

1 Make the basic ground beef as in the recipe, but add the diced green pepper to the onion before frying, and add the corn and chili powder with the soy protein.

2 Meanwhile, make 4 crêpes from the batter. Preheat the oven to 400°F. When the beef is cooked, spoon ¼ of the mixture into the middle of each crêpe and roll them up. Arrange the rolls in a greased shallow dish and sprinkle the grated cheese over them. Bake for 20 minutes until the cheese is melted and golden. Serve immediately.

Serves 4

Beef Brunchies

½ lb. ground beef
3 tablespoons sweet pickle or mango chutney
2 hard-boiled eggs, chopped
4 slices toasted bread
½ cup grated cheese

1 Make the basic ground beef as in the recipe. When cooked, stir in the sweet pickle or chutney and the chopped eggs.

2 Make the toast and spoon ¼ of the beef mixture onto each slice. Sprinkle the grated cheese over them and serve.

Serves 4

Reading clockwise: Stuffed Crêpes, Beef and Vegetable Vol-au-vent, Beef Brunchies and Curried Beef and Golden Rice

Beef España

1 lb. stewing beef

For the Sauce:
2 tablespoons oil
1 medium onion, chopped
2 tablespoons flour
2 tablespoons tomato paste
1 clove garlic, peeled and crushed
1¼ cups water
1 beef bouillon cube
¼ cup medium sherry
salt and pepper
12 green olives, stuffed
sprig rosemary

1 Preheat the oven to 400°F.

2 Slice the boiled beef thickly and place in an ovenproof dish.

3 To make the sauce, heat the oil in a skillet and fry the onion lightly for 5 minutes, until tender and slightly brown. Stir in the flour and cook for 1 minute more. Stir in the tomato paste and garlic and pour on the water. Crumble in the bouillon cube and bring to a boil. Add the sherry and simmer for 15 minutes. Pass the sauce through a strainer.

4 Season to taste. Scatter the olives over the beef, pour on the sauce and place the dish in the oven for 20 minutes. Garnish with a sprig of rosemary and serve hot.

Serves 4

Tip: You can replace the olives with dill pickles or capers.

Spanish Pie

1½ lbs. stewing beef, cut in ¾-inch cubes
¼ cup flour

Beef España is a quick and easy way of using up boiled beef in a sherry-flavored sauce with olives

1 teaspoon salt
pinch pepper
3 tablespoons lard or shortening
2 large onions, finely sliced
2 branches celery, sliced
⅔ cup water
½ beef bouillon cube
¾ cup tomatoes, skinned, seeded and chopped
1 tablespoon tomato paste
20 green olives, stuffed
¾ lb. puff pastry dough
1 egg, beaten

1 Preheat the oven to 325°F.

2 Coat the beef cubes with the flour, seasoned with salt and pepper. Heat the lard in a skillet and quickly brown the meat in it. Remove and place in a casserole. Sauté the onion and celery in the fat for 3 minutes, then add to the meat. Boil the water in a pan and crumble in the ½ bouillon cube. Pour into the casserole and stir in the tomatoes and tomato paste. Cover and cook for 2 hours or until the meat is tender. Take out of the oven, add the olives and check the seasoning. Turn into a 2½-pint pie dish. Leave to cool.

3 Turn the oven up to 425°F.

4 Roll out the puff pastry dough to a thickness of ⅛ inch on a floured board. Place over the pie dish, trim, and seal the edges. Brush with the beaten egg. Make 2 small slits in the center of the pie and bake for 45 minutes.

Serves 6

All about Veal
Veal in Vermouth and Tuna Sauce

Veal is the meat of the young milk-fed calf of up to 3 months in age, although animals of up to 1 year may be sold as veal.

Veal is at its best from May to September. When choosing veal, the flesh should be pale pink, moist, firm and smell pleasant. The fat should be white and slightly pinkish. The connective tissue should be gelatinous (which will disappear during cooking) but not hard or bubbly. If very white meat is desired for a fricassée, or blanquette, the veal may be soaked in salted water to remove the blood, and even bleached with a little lemon juice in the water.

The cuts of veal are similar to those of beef, with chuck, ribs, loin and legs providing the most commonly used cuts. The chuck can be used for roasts, bone-in chops, veal cubes, veal patties, and lower quality cutlets. The ribs can be used for rib chops and high quality roasts such as split veal rack and crown roast. The loin, which includes the loin eye muscle and the tenderloin, provides steaks, loin chops, medallions of veal, and rolled roasts. The legs supply the highest quality veal cutlets, which are pounded and prepared for dishes such as veal scallopine and veal parmigiana, and can also be boned, rolled, and tied for roasting. Shank is used for stews and the famous Osso Buco. Foreshank and breast provide meat for stews and rolled roasts.

The liver and kidneys are renowned for their high quality. Calf's head and feet may be boiled and served with a sharp vinaigrette sauce.

Veal is an expensive meat and is probably best known for the world-famous Wiener Schnitzel. To make a Wiener Schnitzel cutlet, only 3 ozs. of meat are used. It is flattened out and cooked very briefly in a mixture of oil and butter.

The meat has very little fat and tends to be rather bland and lacking in flavor. For this reason, interesting sauces are often made to go with veal, and pot roasting on a bed of vegetables, or braising, is a better, more tasty way to cook veal than a simple roast.

Veal Roasts

Veal in Vermouth and Tuna Sauce

2 lbs. boned rolled leg of veal
2 tablespoons butter
2 tablespoons oil
1¼ cups water

For the Marinade:
2¼ cups dry vermouth
2 tablespoons vinegar
1 large onion, sliced
1 large carrot, sliced
2 cloves garlic, peeled and chopped
salt and pepper
pinch basil

For the Sauce:
5 ozs. tuna
4 anchovy fillets
3 egg yolks
yolks of 2 hard-boiled eggs
juice 1 lemon
1 tablespoon olive oil
½ tablespoon wine vinegar
salt and pepper
1 dill pickle, sliced
2 tablespoons capers

1 Mix the marinade ingredients and leave the veal to marinate for 2 hours. Remove the meat and dry with absorbent paper.

2 Put the butter and oil in a saucepan and brown the meat. Add the marinade and water, bring to a boil and simmer for 1 hour. Allow to cool in the marinade. If convenient, this part may be done the day before.

3 Remove the meat, and wipe it.

4 Strain the marinade and reduce by fast boiling until 1¼ cups remain. Cool.

5 Make the sauce by mixing the tuna fish, anchovy fillets, egg yolks, hard-boiled egg yolks, lemon juice, olive oil and vinegar. Add the marinade and blend to a smooth, thick sauce, in a blender if possible. Season with salt and pepper, and add the pickle and capers.

6 Cut the veal in thin slices, arrange on a dish, and pour on the sauce. Serve with a rice salad.

Serves 6-8

Veal Vesuvio

1 tablespoon butter
2 tablespoons flour
⅔ cup stock
1¼ cups milk
pinch salt, nutmeg, pepper
juice 1 lemon
¼ cup corn kernels
2 lbs. boned rolled breast of veal
6 ozs. sliced ham
few sprigs watercress
salt and pepper
¼ cup oil
1¼ cups water

1 To make the sauce, make a roux and add the stock. Boil for 10 minutes, add the milk, seasoning and lemon juice. Simmer for 5 minutes. Add the corn.

2 Preheat the oven to 400°F.

3 Unroll the meat, spread with the ham slices, reserving one for decoration, and watercress leaves. Spread with half of the sauce and season. Roll the meat and tie with string. Season and brush with oil.

4 Roast the meat for 1 hour. Add 1¼ cups water to the pan, and cook for ½ hour, basting with the liquid. When cooked, place the meat on a dish.

5 Reheat the remaining sauce and pour over the meat. Decorate with the slice of ham and sprigs of watercress.

Serves 6-8

Veal Vesuvio takes some culinary skill, but the end result makes it all very worthwhile

Veal with Lemon Sauce

2 lbs. veal loin, rump or rolled
 boned shoulder
¼ up oil
2 onions, 2 carrots, 2 branches
 celery, diced
2 lemons
1¼ cups stock
pinch thyme
1 bay leaf
salt and pepper
¼ cup sherry
1 teaspoon cornstarch
¼ cup water
pinch caraway seeds

1 Preheat the oven to 375°F.

2 Brown the veal in the oil in a flameproof casserole, then remove the veal.

3 Put the diced onions, carrots and celery in the casserole, and place the meat on top.

4 Add the finely chopped rind of one lemon.

5 Pour the stock, the juice of the 2 lemons, thyme and bay leaf onto the meat and season. Cover and cook in the oven for 1½ hours.

6 Remove the meat and keep warm.

7 Strain off the liquid and reduce it by fast boiling to 1¼ cups. Add the sherry and boil for 5 minutes. Mix the cornstarch and water and use to thicken the sauce.

8 To serve, carve the meat in slices, arrange on a dish with saffron flavored rice and sprinkle the veal

---

Veal with Lemon Sauce is served with savory saffron rice and makes an extra special roast meal

with caraway seeds. Serve the sauce separately.

Serves 8

Creole Veal with Avocados

¼ cup oil
3 lbs. loin of veal, boned
2 onions, sliced
2 carrots, sliced
¼ cup butter
½ cup flour
1 cup milk
1 cup + 2 tablespoons rum
juice 2 lemons
cayenne pepper, salt and pepper
1 lb. puff pastry
1 beaten egg

1 Preheat the oven to 375°F.

2 Heat the oil in a casserole and brown the meat for 10 minutes and remove.

3 Gently sauté the onions and carrots and place the meat on top. Cover and cook for 1½ hours. Cool.

4 Make 1 pint of thick white sauce using the butter, flour, milk and cream but reserving 2 tablespoons of cream. Cool and add 1 mashed avocado and flavor with rum, half the lemon juice, cayenne pepper, salt and pepper.

5 When the meat and sauce are cold, roll out the pastry ¼ inch thick.

6 Preheat the oven to 400°F.

7 Slice the meat in ½-inch slices and sandwich some sauce between. Press together in the shape of the roast and place on the pastry. Brush the pastry with beaten egg, and wrap around the meat. Turn over, and trim the ends. Brush with beaten egg. Decorate with leaves cut from pastry trimmings, and brush with egg. Let rest for 20 minutes, and bake for 25 minutes.

8 Meanwhile, thin the remainder

Veal en Croûte, in its succulent pastry, is an impressive dish to serve at dinner parties

of the sauce with the remainder of the lemon juice and cream.

9 Just before serving, garnish the roast with slices of avocado. Serve cold with the sauce.

Serves 8

Veal en Croûte

1½ lbs. loin of veal
¼ cup oil
salt and pepper

To make the Flavored Paste:
6 ozs. calves liver
1 large onion
6 ozs. mushrooms
1 egg
1 cup breadcrumbs
1 clove garlic, chopped
1 tablespoon parsley
salt and pepper
1 lb. puff pastry
1 beaten egg

1 Preheat the oven to 400°F.

2 Brush the loin of veal with oil. Season with salt and pepper and place in a roasting pan. Roast for 1 hour. Cool.

3 To make the flavored paste, remove the skin from the raw calves liver and grind. Chop the onion and mushrooms finely, and mix with the egg, breadcrumbs, garlic, parsley and seasoning. Mix with the liver to a smooth paste.

4 When the meat is cold, roll the pastry to an oblong ¼ inch thick. Place the veal in the middle and brush with beaten egg. Spread the paste thickly over it. Brush the pastry with beaten egg. Wrap around the meat with a wide overlap. Turn over so that the seam is underneath, and trim off the ends, making a loaf shape.

5 Place on a greased tray, and brush the outside with beaten egg. Roll out the trimmings to make leaves and place on top for decoration, brushing again with beaten egg. Let rest for 20 minutes.

6 Bake for 25 minutes. Serve hot or cold.

Serves 6

Braised Veal in Mushroom Sauce

2½ lbs. boned and rolled veal roast (leg or shoulder)
6 tablespoons butter
2 shallots, chopped
2 onions, chopped
1 sprig thyme
1 bay leaf
salt and pepper
1⅓ cups cider
½ lb. mushrooms, chopped
1 egg yolk
½ cup light cream
2 tablespoons chopped parsley

1 Fry the veal gently in ¼ cup of the butter until browned on all sides. Lift out. Sauté the shallots and onions in the same fat until softened.

2 Return the veal to the pan and add the thyme, bay leaf, salt and pepper to taste and the cider. Bring to a boil, cover and cook over low heat for 1½ hours.

3 Fry the mushrooms in the rest of the butter for 3-4 minutes.

4 When the veal has cooked for 1½ hours, add the mushrooms to the pan and continue cooking for a further 10 minutes.

5 Drain the veal and place on a serving dish. Keep warm. Discard the thyme and bay leaf.

6 Beat the egg yolk with the cream. Beat into the cooking liquid and cook gently until thickened. Cover the meat with this sauce, sprinkle with the parsley and serve hot.

Serves 6

Roast Veal Steaks Parisienne

2 lbs. loin of veal, cut in 6 steaks
salt and pepper
¼ lb. butter
1¼ cups dry white wine
5 potatoes, cut into balls
6 small onions
½ cup light cream
2 slices cooked ham, diced
3 cups fresh mushrooms, cooked, diced
6 cooked artichoke hearts
sprig parsley, chopped

1 Preheat the oven to 400°F. Season the veal steaks and spread them with half of the butter. Cook in the oven for ½ hour, turning once to brown both sides. During the cooking, use the wine to baste the meat.

2 Meanwhile, fry the potato balls and onions, covered, in the rest of the butter for 10 minutes. Drain and keep hot.

3 When the meat is cooked, drain the gravy into a pan and bring to a boil. Add the cream and boil for 5 minutes. Season.

4 Place the steaks on an ovenproof dish and pour a little of the sauce on. Mix the ham and mushrooms and pile on top of the artichoke hearts. Arrange these around the meat and place in the oven for 12 minutes to heat through.

5 Decorate the dish with the potato and onions and sprinkle with the parsley. Serve the rest of the sauce separately.

Serves 6

Shoulder of Veal in Vermouth

3 lbs. boned shoulder of veal
¼ cup brandy
salt and pepper
¼ cup milk
2 cups fresh breadcrumbs
5 ozs. cream cheese
1 cup finely chopped mushrooms
½ lb. chopped cooked ham
1 tablespoon chopped parsley
1 large clove garlic, chopped
2 onions, chopped
1 egg
1½ tablespoons butter
2 tablespoons oil
1¼ cups dry white vermouth
⅔ cup light cream

1 Place the veal in a dish, spoon on the brandy and season with salt and pepper. Let marinate, turning once.

2 Pour the milk over the breadcrumbs. Let it soak in, then squeeze the bread dry.

3 Put the cream cheese, mushrooms, ham, breadcrumbs, parsley, garlic and onions in a bowl. Add the egg and season with salt and pepper. Mix thoroughly.

4 Spread this stuffing thinly over the inside of the veal. Roll up and tie securely with kitchen string.

5 Heat the butter and oil in a large pan. Add the meat and brown on all sides. Add the vermouth, cover and leave to cook over low heat for about 1½ hours.

6 Place the meat on a heated serving dish and keep hot.

7 Add the cream to the pan. Mix quickly with a wooden spoon over a brisk heat. Correct the seasoning, pour the sauce into a sauce boat and serve with the veal.

Serves 7-8

For Extra Flavor
The delicate flavor of veal can be enhanced by cooking it with aromatic vegetables such as carrots, celery and onions, and with fragrant herbs including basil, rosemary and marjoram. To add flavor to the gravy served with veal roasts, you may use veal stock, but may also try incorporating dry white wine, sherry or even vermouth for a really impressive sauce.

Roast Veal Steaks Parisienne are garnished with artichoke hearts topped with ham and mushrooms

Cutlets and Steaks

Veal cutlets, which come from the leg of the calf, are considered particularly choice cuts since they contain no fat or gristle. They are cut about ¼ inch thick and are then usually beaten with a mallet or rolling pin until very thin.

Scaloppines and cutlets are similar cuts of veal but differ in the way in which they are cut from the main joint: scaloppines are cut against the grain of the meat whereas cutlets are cut with it.

We have included in this section one recipe which uses veal loin steaks. The loin is a prime cut and so the steaks can be very expensive; pork loin steaks would make a suitable alternative, but the cooking time should be lengthened to ensure that the meat is cooked through.

Veal Steaks with Jerusalem Artichokes

¼ cup oil
¼ cup butter
Six ½-lb. veal loin steaks, ½ inch thick

For the Sauce:
1 onion, chopped
bouquet garni
⅔ cup dry vermouth
1 bouillon cube
⅔ cup water
juice ½ lemon
1½ tablespoons cornstarch

For the Garnish:
¼ cup butter
2 lbs. Jerusalem artichokes, cut in halves
1 onion, chopped

1 Heat the oil and butter in a pan, add the veal steaks and cook for 12-14 minutes over low heat and covered with a lid. Turn the steaks over once or twice during the cooking time. Remove the steaks and keep them warm.

2 Make the sauce. Using the fat left from cooking the meat, sauté the onion for 5 minutes and then remove surplus fat. Add the bouquet garni and vermouth and boil for 8 minutes.

3 Dissolve the bouillon cube in the water, add the stock to the pan and boil for 4 minutes more. Season to taste and add the lemon juice.

4 Mix the cornstarch with 6 tablespoons water and add to the sauce. Boil for 1 minute until thickened. Strain the sauce and pour a little of the sauce over the veal.

5 For the garnish, heat the butter in a pan and sauté the Jerusalem artichokes for 6 minutes, covered with a lid. Add the chopped onion and cook for 2 minutes more. Drain off the fat, add ½ cup of the sauce and simmer for 5 minutes. Season.

6 Serve the veal steaks with the garnish and pour the rest of the sauce into a sauce boat.

Serves 6

Wiener Schnitzel

4 veal cutlets
6 tablespoons flour, lightly salted
1 egg, beaten
¾ cup fine dried breadcrumbs
¼ cup butter
4 slices lemon

1 Place the veal cutlets between 2 sheets of dampened parchment paper and beat with a mallet or rolling pin until very thin, ⅛ inch thick.

2 Coat the veal with the seasoned flour, then dip in the beaten egg and the breadcrumbs until thoroughly coated.

3 Melt the butter in a large skillet. Add the veal and fry over moderate heat until golden-brown on both sides, turning once during cooking.

4 Transfer the veal to a warm serving dish and serve immediately, garnished with the lemon slices. Serve with new potatoes tossed in parsley and a green salad.

Serves 4

Veal Cutlets in Marsala

4 veal cutlets
¼ cup butter
½ cup Marsala
¾ cup gravy or thickened stock
pinch cayenne pepper

1 Place the veal cutlets between 2 sheets of dampened parchment and beat with a mallet or rolling pin until they are ⅛ inch thick.

2 Heat the butter in a skillet and fry the cutlets until well browned. Transfer them to a warm serving dish and keep hot.

3 Add the Marsala to the fat in the pan and boil for 5 minutes, stirring well. Add the gravy or stock and cayenne, mix well and pour the sauce over the veal.

Serves 4

Veal Cutlets Milanese

8 asparagus spears
4 veal cutlets

$\frac{1}{4}$ **cup butter**
1 teaspoon cornstarch
$\frac{1}{4}$ **cup port**
3 tablespoons light cream
sprig tarragon, finely chopped
pinch paprika
salt and pepper

1 Cook the asparagus in boiling salted water for 15-20 minutes.

2 Meanwhile, place the veal cutlets between 2 sheets of dampened parchment paper and beat with a mallet or rolling pin until very thin. Heat the butter in a skillet and fry the cutlets over low heat for 5-8

Veal Steaks with Jerusalem Artichokes is a dish that shows how well veal combines with less familiar vegetables

minutes on each side or until cooked through.

3 Mix the cornstarch and the port. Drain the cutlets and arrange them on a heated serving dish. Keep hot.

4 Pour the cream into the skillet and stir well to mix with the pan juices. Add the tarragon. Boil for 2

minutes, then add the cornstarch mixed with the port. Simmer, stirring, until thickened. Add the paprika and the salt and pepper to taste.

5 Drain the asparagus and arrange around the cutlets. Pour the sauce over the top and serve very hot.

Serves 4

Tip: The asparagus must be very carefully drained to ensure that no extra water is added to the sauce—otherwise it will become diluted.

Veal Rib Chops

Veal rib chops can be either broiled or fried. It is important to differentiate between rib chops and loin chops— many people confuse the two. Rib chops are taken from the best rib part of the animal and usually weigh about 10 ozs. and are $\frac{1}{2}$ inch thick. Frying is the best method of cooking them. Season the rib chops with salt and pepper, dredge with flour and brown the rib chops on both sides. Then fry gently, covered with a lid, for 15 minutes. Use clarified butter or oil and butter mixed for the best results and flavor. When the rib chops are cooked, drain off the butter, remove the rib chops and pour a little white wine, sherry or Madeira into the pan. Add some rich brown sauce with sliced cooked mushrooms and boil for 5 minutes. Serve with the rib chops.

Veal Cutlets Provençale

4 tomatoes
salt and pepper
3 tablespoons olive oil
four $\frac{1}{2}$ lb. veal cutlets
$\frac{1}{2}$ cup flour
$\frac{1}{4}$ lb. butter
$\frac{1}{3}$ cup green olives, pitted and blanched
1 clove garlic, peeled and crushed
1 bunch parsley, chopped

1 Preheat the oven to 375°F.

2 Wash the tomatoes and place them in an ovenproof dish. Sprinkle with salt and pepper and pour in the oil. Place in the oven for about 10 minutes.

3 Tenderize the cutlets by beating with a mallet or rolling pin. Season with salt and pepper and dredge with flour.

4 Melt half of the butter in a skillet and fry the cutlets for about 5 minutes on each side until browned and cooked.

5 Arrange the cutlets in a dish, place the olives and baked tomatoes around the edges. Keep warm.

6 Melt the rest of the butter in a pan and sauté the garlic and parsley for a minute, stirring all the time. Pour this butter mixture over the cutlets and serve at once.

Serves 4

Veal Rib Chops with Mushrooms

$\frac{1}{4}$ lb. butter
$3\frac{3}{4}$ cups sliced mushrooms
salt and pepper
four $\frac{1}{2}$ lb. veal rib chops
2 tablespoons brandy
$\frac{1}{2}$ cup light cream
1 tablespoon chopped parsley

1 Melt the butter in a skillet. Add the sliced mushrooms and salt and pepper and fry until tender. Remove from the pan and keep warm.

2 Season the rib chops with salt and pepper and place in the pan. Fry gently until browned on both sides and cooked through.

3 Warm the brandy and pour it over the chops. Ignite and, when the flames die down, transfer the chops to a heated serving dish and keep warm.

4 Add the cream to the pan and boil for 2 minutes to thicken, stirring all the time. Taste the sauce and correct the seasoning.

5 Arrange the mushrooms around the veal chops. Pour the sauce over the chops and sprinkle with the chopped parsley. Serve very hot with sautéed potatoes.

Serves 4

Tip: Veal rib chops are delicious when dredged with flour and fried and served on a bed of green beans, as shown in the picture. Pour the butter and meat juices over the veal and sprinkle with chopped parsley. This makes a very quick and easy meal to prepare.

Veal Chops Portuguese

six $\frac{1}{2}$ lb. veal rib chops
salt and pepper
$\frac{1}{2}$ cup flour
$\frac{1}{4}$ cup oil
1 onion, sliced
1 red pepper, seeded and sliced
2 tomatoes, skinned, seeded and chopped
2 cloves garlic, peeled and chopped
pinch rosemary
$\frac{1}{2}$ cup corn kernels
$\frac{2}{3}$ cup dry sherry
$\frac{2}{3}$ cup water
1 chicken bouillon cube
salt and pepper
pinch paprika

1 Sprinkle the rib chops with salt and pepper and dredge with flour. Heat the oil in a skillet and fry the chops for 5 minutes on each side until browned. Transfer the chops to a shallow ovenproof dish and keep warm.

2 Preheat the oven to 375°F.

3 Sauté the onion in the same pan for 5 minutes until soft. Add the sliced pepper and fry for a further 2 minutes. Add the tomatoes, garlic, rosemary and corn and stir well. Pour in the sherry and water and sprinkle in the bouillon cube. Season with salt and pepper and paprika, and boil for 5 minutes.

4 Pour the sauce over the veal and braise gently in the oven for 35 minutes, covered with a lid. Serve with plain boiled rice.

Serves 6

Veal Chops Bonne Femme

four ½-lb. veal rib chops
salt and pepper
½ cup flour
¼ lb. clarified butter or butter and oil mixed
2 small boiled, cold potatoes, thinly sliced
1 cup pearl onions
½ cup sherry
⅔ cup rich brown sauce
1 tablespoon chopped parsley

Veal rib chops look as good as they taste if served with a colorful vegetable, such as these tender green beans

1 Sprinkle the rib chops with the salt and pepper and dredge with flour.

2 Preheat the oven to 400°F.

3 Heat the butter in a skillet and gently fry the rib chops on both sides for a few minutes.

4 Place the rib chops on an ovenproof dish in the oven to continue cooking.

5 Fry the potatoes in the same pan until golden-brown, remove and keep warm. Then sauté the onions for 2 minutes. Transfer the onions to a saucepan of water and boil until soft.

6 Drain off the butter and pour the sherry into the pan. Add the brown sauce and bring to a boil, stirring all the time.

7 Arrange the rib chops on a serving dish, surrounded by the fried potatoes and onions. Cover with the sauce and sprinkle with chopped parsley.

Serves 4

Stuffed Veal

These dishes use cutlets in a different way by stuffing them with interesting fillings, rolling them up into little parcels, and then gently braising them. The long slow cooking means that it is not necessary to use expensive cuts and the cutlets can be cut from any part, such as the chuck.

Veal Paupiettes

5 ozs. lean pork or veal trimmings
1 egg
1¼ cups slightly whipped all-
　purpose cream
4 veal cutlets, 6 ozs. each
salt, pepper, and nutmeg
2 tablespoons butter
¾ cup white wine

1 Chop and grind the pork or veal trimmings. Put in a bowl, add the egg and mix well. Stir in ¼ cup of the cream and chill to make a firm paste.

2 On a wet board, beat the cutlets to make them very thin. Season with salt, pepper and nutmeg.

3 Spread the stuffing on the cutlets, roll up and tie with string.

4 Heat the butter and brown the paupiettes all over.

5 Add the rest of the cream and the white wine and stir carefully. Bring to a boil and simmer the paupiettes for 1 hour.

6 Remove the paupiettes. Discard the string and keep hot.

7 Reduce the sauce to 1¼ cups by fast boiling, and pour over the paupiettes.

Serves 4

Hungarian Veal Paupiettes

½ cup sausage meat
½ cup ground ham
1 egg
salt and pepper
6 cutlets, ¼ lb. each
½ cup flour
¼ cup oil
1 lb. carrots
¼ lb. lean bacon
¼ cup butter
¾ cup white wine
½ lb. pearl onions
1¼ cups stock
1 tablespoon chopped parsley

1 Blend the sausage meat, ham, egg and seasoning to a smooth paste. Chill.

2 On a wet board, flatten the cutlets by beating to make them thin. Spread the filling on each cutlet. Roll up and tie with string, and dip in flour.

3 Heat half of the oil in a pan and brown the paupiettes for 4 minutes, covered with a lid. Remove and put in a casserole.

4 Slice the carrots. Cut the bacon into strips.

5 Heat the butter and rest of the oil and fry the bacon for 1 minute, then add the carrots. Sauté for 3 minutes, then add the bacon and carrots to the veal.

6 Add the white wine and bring to a boil. Cover the dish and simmer for 1 hour.

7 Meanwhile, boil the pearl onions in stock for 2 minutes.

8 Remove the paupiettes, discard the string.

9 Reduce the sauce by fast boiling to 1¼ cups.

10 Serve the paupiettes surrounded by the bacon, carrots and onions. Pour on the sauce. Sprinkle with parsley.

Serves 6

Veal with Olives

2 large onions, chopped
¼ cup butter
¼ lb. calves liver
¼ lb. lean bacon
1 cup olives, pitted
¼ lb. veal trimmings
1 cup breadcrumbs
1 egg
salt and pepper
6 veal cutlets, 6 ozs. each
1 carrot, chopped
1 tablespoon flour
½ cup white wine
1 cup stock
2 tablespoons tomato paste
bouquet garni

1 Sauté one chopped onion in 2 tablespoons of the butter and brown lightly. Put in a bowl. Briefly fry the calves liver to brown and remove.

2 Mince the bacon, one third of the olives, veal trimmings and liver, and add to the onions. Add the breadcrumbs and egg.

3 On a wet board, beat the cutlets to make them thin. Spread with the stuffing. Roll up and tie with string.

4 Brown the paupiettes all over in the remainder of the butter. Remove and put in a casserole.

5 Add the other chopped onion and carrot and brown. Stir in the flour and brown. Add the white wine, stock and tomato paste. Add the bouquet garni, salt and pepper.

6 Pour over the paupiettes and cook for 1 hour. Add the remainder of the olives 10 minutes before the end.

7 Remove the paupiettes. Discard the string, and arrange on a dish. Reduce the sauce to 1¼ cups and pour over.

Serves 6

Hungarian Veal Paupiettes, stuffed with sausage meat, wins compliments from guests at the dinner table

Look 'n Cook Veal Paupiettes

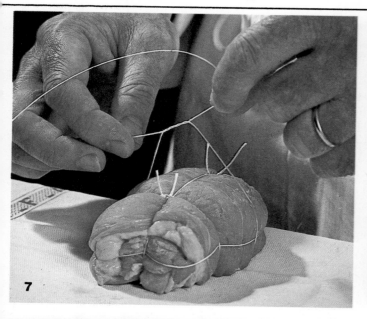

1 Chop the lean pork or veal trimmings to be used for the stuffing and put through a grinder **2** Place in a bowl and keep cool over ice cubes or chill in a refrigerator when made. Add 1 egg and season with salt and freshly ground pepper **3** Add the cream gradually and stir to make a smooth firm paste and chill until used **4** On a wet board, beat the cutlets until they are very thin **5** Place on a cloth to dry and then spread the chilled stuffing carefully on each cutlet **6** Roll up tightly **7** Tie up securely with string into neat parcels **8** Heat a mixture of butter and oil and brown the paupiettes all over, covered with a lid **9** Add the cream and white wine. Stir carefully, season and add a bouquet garni, bring to a boil and simmer for 1 hour **10** When the paupiettes are tender, remove from the pan. Carefully remove all the string and arrange on a dish. Reduce the sauce by fast boiling to 1¼ cups and check the seasoning and pour over the paupiettes and serve hot

Veal Stews

Blanquette de Veau

2 lbs. stewing veal from neck or
 shoulder
salt and pepper
2 large carrots
1 large leek
1 branch celery
2 cloves garlic
bouquet garni
1 onion studded with 2 cloves
$\frac{1}{4}$ lb. butter
$\frac{1}{2}$ cup flour
1 lb. small onions
1 lb. mushrooms
juice $\frac{1}{2}$ lemon
2 egg yolks
$\frac{2}{3}$ cup heavy cream
pinch nutmeg

1 Cut the veal into 1½-inch cubes.
Place in a saucepan, cover with cold
water and bring to a boil. Drain and
rinse in cold water, removing any
scum. Return the meat to the pan,
cover with water, season with salt
and pepper. Bring to a boil, then
simmer.

2 Slice the carrots in 4 lengthwise,
trim and clean the leek, chop the
celery and garlic. Add these vegetables, with the bouquet garni and
the onion studded with 2 cloves, to
the meat. Cover and simmer gently
for 1¼ hours.

3 Make a roux with half of the butter, and the flour. Cook for 2
minutes and leave to cool.

4 Sauté the small onions in half of
the remaining butter. Blanch the
mushrooms in the other half of the
butter, the lemon juice and 2 tablespoons water, until tender. The
liquor may be added to the stew.

5 Take the meat from the pan and
keep warm. Remove the vegetables

and strain the sauce. Pour some of
the liquid onto the roux and blend
to produce a thin, smooth sauce.
Bring to a boil, adjust seasoning.

6 In another bowl beat together
the egg yolks and cream with a
pinch of nutmeg. Stir in ½ cup of the
sauce. Pour this mixture into the
stew sauce, stirring briskly with a
sauce whisk to a thick, smooth
sauce.

7 Return meat, mushrooms and
small onions to a pan and pour the
sauce over them through a sieve.
Reheat without bringing to a boil.
Arrange the meat and vegetables in
a heated serving dish, pour the
sauce over them, and serve hot.

Serves 8

Veal Fricassée

2 onions, chopped
1½ lbs. stewing veal cut in 1¼-inch
 cubes
$\frac{2}{3}$ cup white wine
1 bay leaf
pinch thyme
salt and pepper
$\frac{1}{4}$ cup flour
2 tablespoons butter
2 tablespoons milk
$\frac{1}{4}$ lb. mushrooms

1 Preheat oven to 325°F. Place the
veal, onions, wine, herbs, and
seasoning to taste in a casserole,
cover and cook in the oven for
about 1¼ hours or until the meat is
tender. Remove the meat, strain
liquid.

2 Make a roux of the flour and
butter and cook for 2 minutes.
Remove from the heat, add the
milk to make a smooth paste, and
stir in the cooking liquid to make
up 1¼ cups of smooth sauce.

3 Pour the sauce over the veal in
the casserole, add the mushrooms,
and return to the oven for 20
minutes. Serve hot.

Serves 4

Mediterranean Veal Stew

1½ lbs. shoulder veal cut in 1¼-inch
 cubes
3 onions, chopped
3 tablespoons oil
$\frac{1}{4}$ cup flour
juice 1 lemon
1¼ cups white meat stock
2 cloves garlic, peeled and
 chopped
1 lb. tomatoes, skinned, seeded
 and chopped
2 green peppers, seeded and
 sliced
2 cups peas
salt and pepper
$\frac{2}{3}$ cup pitted green olives
$\frac{1}{2}$ cup light cream

1 Fry the meat and onions in the
oil until lightly browned. Add the
flour and stir while cooking for 2
minutes.

2 Stir in the lemon juice, stock,
garlic, tomatoes, green peppers,
peas and seasoning to taste. Bring
to a boil, cover and simmer gently
for 25 minutes.

3 Dip the olives into boiling water
for 1 minute, drain and chop them
roughly. Add them to the pan and
continue to cook for 15 minutes.

4 Remove the meat and vegetables
and transfer them to a heated serving dish. Add the cream to the pan
and boil, stirring constantly, for 5
minutes to thicken. Pour the sauce
over the meat and serve at once.

Serves 4

Serbian Veal with Yogurt

2 green peppers, seeded and
 diced
2 tablespoons oil
1½ lbs. shoulder veal

Look 'n Cook Blanching Mushrooms

1 Cut a lemon in two and squeeze the juice out **2** Put the butter into a heavy-based saucepan. Break it into pieces with a wooden spoon. Pour in the lemon juice. Melt the butter, stirring. Do not allow the mixture to brown **3** Add the turned mushroom heads and the water. Simmer gently without a lid **4** When the mushrooms are tender, remove them from the pan

---

2 large onions, quartered
¼ cup shortening
salt and pepper
1 cup white meat stock
1 tablespoon paprika
4 large tomatoes, peeled, seeded and chopped
1¼ cups yogurt

1 Sauté the diced green peppers in the oil for 10-15 minutes over low heat.

2 Cut the meat into ¼-inch slices. In a saucepan, sauté the veal and onions in the shortening until lightly browned. Season with salt and pepper, pour in the stock, add the paprika and bring to a boil. Cover and simmer for 20 minutes.

3 Add the tomatoes to the green peppers and cook for 10 minutes over low heat, stirring constantly.

4 Remove the veal and onion from the saucepan, leaving the liquid, and place in a warm serving dish. Strain the green pepper and tomato, arrange around the meat, and pour any remaining vegetable liquid into the meat liquor.

5 Stir the yogurt into the liquor over heat, and beat for 2 minutes with a whisk. Pour over the veal.

Serves 4

Look 'n Cook Blanquette de Veau

1 Place veal in a saucepan, cover with cold water and bring to a boil **2** Drain and rinse in cold water. Return veal to pan, cover with water and season. Bring to a boil **3** Slice carrots, trim and clean leek, prepare onion, bouquet garni, celery, garlic. Add vegetables to meat and simmer 1¼ hours **4** Make a roux from the butter and flour. Cook 2 minutes and let cool **5** Sauté the small onions in butter **6** Poach the mushrooms in butter, water and lemon juice until soft. Add the liquor to the stew **7** Remove meat from pan and reserve. Dis-

card vegetables. Strain cooking liquor through a sieve
8 Pour part of the liquor on the roux. Bring to a boil, stirring, and add more liquor if needed to make a smooth thin sauce **9** Mix cream and egg yolks with some of the sauce. Add to the sauce, beating to thicken

10 Combine meat, mushrooms and onions and pour the sauce over them through a sieve. Reheat without boiling **11** and **12** Place meat mixture in a dish, pour on the sauce and serve hot

Veal Marengo

2 lbs. stewing veal (from the
  shoulder)
¼ cup oil
¼ cup butter
2 large onions, finely chopped
½ cup flour
1¼ cups white wine
4 tomatoes, skinned, seeded and
  chopped
2 cloves garlic, crushed
bouquet garni
salt and pepper
1 lb. scallions
1 tablespoon butter
1 tablespoon sugar
3 cups mushrooms
4 slices white bread
1 tablespoon chopped parsley

1 Cut the veal into 1-inch cubes.
Brown it quickly in half the oil and
butter, mixed. Add the chopped
onions and cook them gently with
the meat until soft. Dust with flour
and cook until it just browns.

2 Add the white wine and stir to
absorb any juices which are stuck
onto the pan. Mix in the tomatoes,
garlic and bouquet garni, cover
with water, and season with salt
and pepper. Bring to a boil, cover
the pan and simmer over low heat
for 1-1¼ hours.

3 Peel the scallion bulbs, cutting
away the green leaves, and sauté
bulbs to light golden in the butter
and sugar.

4 Quarter the mushrooms and fry
them gently in the other half of the
oil and butter mixture.

5 Cut the bread into heart-shaped
croûtons, and fry them until crisp
and golden-brown in the rest of the
oil and butter.

6 Add the scallions and mushrooms to the meat and simmer for 5
minutes more. Chop the parsley
and dip the pointed end of each
croûton in the meat sauce and then

in the parsley. Serve in a deep,
heated dish, garnished with the
croûtons.

Serves 8

Veal Shoulder Riviera
with Noodles

1½ lbs. veal shoulder in 2-
  inch thick pieces
6 ozs. veal kidney, sliced
¼ cup oil
1 large onion, chopped
3 carrots, scraped and sliced
2 branches celery, sliced
⅔ cup white wine
⅔ cup white meat stock
1 clove garlic, crushed
2 cups noodles
¼ cup butter
⅓ cup grated Parmesan
salt and pepper
¼ cup light cream
large pinch paprika
parsley to garnish

1 Brown the veal shoulder and
kidney in the oil for 8 minutes,
turning the shoulder pieces once.
Add the vegetables, cover and
simmer gently for 10 minutes.

2 Pour in the wine and stock, add
the garlic and season to taste. Simmer for 1½ hours.

3 Boil the noodles in salted water
for 8-10 minutes until tender. Drain
them and stir in the butter,
Parmesan cheese, and a pinch of
salt and pepper.

4 Stir the cream and paprika into
the meat mixture. Bring back to a
boil and remove from heat.

5 Arrange the noodles around a
heated serving dish and fill the center with the meat and sauce. Garnish with sprigs of parsley, and
serve at once.

Serves 4

Crêpes Corsican Style

2 eggs
1 cup flour
1¼ cups milk
¼ cup butter
1 large onion, chopped
½ cup diced mushrooms
¾ cup ground cooked veal
pinch curry powder
1 clove garlic, chopped
1 tablespoon tomato paste
1 tablespoon flour
salt and pepper
pinch oregano

For the Sauce:
1 egg yolk
1 teaspoon prepared mustard
1¼ cups white sauce
½ cup grated cheese
pinch paprika

1 Combine the eggs, flour and
milk into a smooth batter and make
6 crêpes, about 6 inches wide.

2 Melt the butter and sauté the
chopped onion for 5 minutes until
soft. Add the mushrooms and sauté
for 1 minute. Blend in the ground
veal, curry powder, garlic, tomato
paste, flour, salt and pepper to
taste, and oregano. Cook gently for
8 minutes, and leave to cool.

3 Divide the mixture between the
crêpes. Roll up each crêpe and
place in a a shallow ovenproof dish.

4 Blend the egg yolk and mustard
and mix in the white sauce. Stir in ¾
of the grated cheese, and season
with salt, pepper and a pinch of
paprika. Pour the sauce over the
crêpes, sprinkle on the rest of the
cheese, and place dish under the
broiler until browned. Serve hot.

Serves 3

---

*Veal Shoulder Riviera with
Noodles (left), and Crêpes
Corsican Style (right) are two
tasty ideas for lunch*

7

8

9

10

1 The main ingredients: veal, bread, tomatoes, onions, mushrooms, herbs and garlic **2** Cut the veal into cubes and brown quickly in oil and butter **3** Cook the chopped onions gently with the meat **4** Dust with flour and cook gently to brown **5** Add the white wine and stir to absorb any juices stuck to the pan. Add tomatoes, garlic, bouquet garni and hot water to cover, and season. Bring to a boil, cover and simmer for 1-1¼ hours **6** Peel the scallion bulbs and brown in butter and sugar **7** Clean the mushrooms, quarter and sauté them in butter **8** Cut the bread into heart-shaped croûtons. Fry to golden-brown **9** Add the mushrooms and scallions to the meat and simmer for 5 minutes. Chop the parsley **10** Serve in a deep, heated serving dish. Dip the point of each croûton in the sauce and then in the chopped parsley. Arrange the croûtons around the dish. Serve very hot

Osso Buco with Artichoke Hearts

2 tablespoons flour
salt and pepper
8 slices veal shank 1 inch thick
2 tablespoons butter
1 large onion, sliced
2 cloves garlic, peeled and crushed
2 carrots, sliced
2 branches celery, finely chopped
¾ cup dry white wine
4 large tomatoes, skinned, seeded and chopped
1 tablespoon tomato paste
1 bay leaf
pinch dried rosemary
8 canned artichoke hearts
juice and grated peel 1 lemon
1 tablespoon chopped parsley

1 Season the flour with salt and pepper. Dredge the veal in it. Heat the butter in a skillet and brown the veal. Take out and place in a heavy-based pan.

2 Lightly sauté the onion, garlic, carrots and celery in the oil, then add to the meat.

3 Pour the wine over the meat and vegetables. Bring to a boil, then lower heat to simmering. Stir in the tomatoes, tomato paste, bay leaf and rosemary. Season to taste. Cover and let simmer for 1 hour or until the meat is tender.

4 Add the drained artichoke hearts and the juice and grated rind of the lemon. Cook for 10 minutes more. Immediately before serving, sprinkle on the chopped parsley. Serve with plain boiled potatoes, rice or noodles and a crisp green salad.

Serves 4

Tips: This dish can also be made using veal shank cut 2 inches thick. Allow one per portion and cook for 1½ hours.

The marrow inside the shinbone is delicious: eat it with the stew.

Shoulder of Veal Paysanne

20 pearl onions
20 small carrots
salt and pepper
3 lbs. shoulder of veal cut in 2-inch pieces
¼ cup flour
2 tablespoons butter
1½ cups water
1 chicken bouillon cube
bouquet garni
20 small new potatoes
1 lb. green peas, fresh or frozen

1 Carefully peel the onions, leaving them whole. Peel and trim the carrots.

2 Season the veal and dredge in the flour. Heat the butter in a skillet and brown the meat in it. Transfer to a heavy-based stewing pan. Sauté the onions and carrots in the butter for 1 minute, then add to the meat.

3 Pour on the water, crumble in the bouillon cube and bring to a boil. Reduce heat at once, add the bouquet garni and check seasoning. Cover and simmer gently for 30 minutes.

4 Peel the new potatoes and add them to the pan with the peas. Add more stock, if necessary, so the vegetables are just covered. Replace the lid on the pan and simmer again for 45 minutes to 1 hour, until the meat is tender.

Serves 6

Veal Hotpot

1½ lbs. leg of veal
¼ lb. bacon
2 medium potatoes
1 medium carrot
1 large onion

1 green or red pepper
1 clove garlic
4 tomatoes
salt and pepper
2 tablespoons flour
2 tablespoons oil
1 tablespoon tomato paste
bouquet garni
pinch paprika
2½ cups water
1 chicken bouillon cube

1 Preheat the oven to 350°F.

2 Cut the veal and the bacon into 2-inch cubes. Peel and quarter the potatoes and carrot. Slice the onion and seed the pepper, cutting it into 2-inch strips. Peel and crush the garlic. Skin, seed and quarter the tomatoes.

3 Season the veal and dredge in the flour. Heat the oil in a skillet and fry the meat until browned. Remove and place in a casserole. Lightly fry the bacon, onion and pepper. Add the garlic, potatoes and carrot and fry for 2 minutes more. Transfer to the casserole.

4 Stir in the tomatoes, tomato paste, the bouquet garni and the paprika. Bring the water to a boil in a pan, crumble in the bouillon cube, and pour over the meat. Cover tightly and place in the oven for about 1 hour or until the veal is tender.

Serves 4-5

Using Pork Shoulder
Dishes which use shoulder or leg of veal can be made more interesting by using half the quantity of veal and making up the difference with pork shoulder. This shoulder has a higher proportion of meat to bone for the same weight and so will work out more economically. Pork and veal combine well together, the pork adding a considerable amount of flavor while the veal supplies the gelatinous ingredient necessary for a good gravy.

Osso Buco is a traditional veal stew from Italy, usually garnished with parsley, lemon and garlic

Veal Kidneys

Veal kidneys are the most delicious kidneys of all. To prepare kidneys, always snip off the white membrane and fat with a pair of scissors, then wash well. Always cook veal kidneys for as short a time as possible over medium heat and *never* overcook. The inside and center of the kidneys should always be very slightly pink. Calves kidneys can be sliced for frying or broiling, or cooked whole in a sauce or casserole.

Sautéed Kidneys and Mushrooms

1 lb. veal kidneys
salt and pepper
¼ cup butter
½ lb. mushrooms
½ cup white wine
⅔ cup rich brown sauce
juice ½ lemon

1 Trim the kidneys, removing the fat and membranes and cut into pieces. Season with salt and pepper.

2 Heat the butter in a skillet and sauté the kidneys for about 5 minutes. Remove and keep warm.

3 Add the mushrooms and sauté for 3 minutes. Add the wine and boil to reduce it, then add the brown sauce. Boil it for a few minutes, stirring from time to time. Stir in the kidneys and the lemon juice. Serve with plain boiled rice and zucchini and broiled tomatoes.

Serves 4

Veal Kidneys in Red Wine

2 carrots
4 onions
6 sprigs parsley
2 celery branches
¼ cup butter
2 tablespoons flour
1¼ cups red wine
¼ cup water
salt
12 peppercorns, crushed
1 clove garlic
pinch thyme
1 bay leaf
1½ lbs. veal kidneys
¼ cup oil

1 Dice the carrots, 2 of the onions, celery, and parsley sprigs. Put 2 tablespoons of butter in a casserole and cook gently without coloring for 2 minutes. Sprinkle on the flour and stir for 1 minute. Add ½ cup of the red wine, and the water. Bring to a boil. Season with salt, crushed peppercorns, crushed garlic, thyme and bay leaf. Simmer for 30 minutes until the vegetables are tender.

2 Prepare the kidneys by removing the skin from the outside. Cut off any fat, and the central hard white core. Slice the kidneys.

3 Heat the oil in a skillet and sauté the slices of kidney briefly. Lift out of the pan, discarding the cooking fat and juices.

4 Heat the remaining butter in a casserole, gently sauté the rest of the onions, chopped finely. Add the rest of the wine and boil until almost evaporated.

5 Add the cooked vegetables and sauce and simmer together for 5 minutes.

6 Sieve the sauce through a conical strainer, pressing the cooked vegetables through the holes or work through a food mill.

7 Pour over the kidneys and reheat without boiling.

8 Put in a serving dish and sprinkle with chopped parsley.

Serves 4

Sweet and Sour Veal Spaghetti

½ lb. spaghetti
2 tablespoons butter
⅓ cup oil
½ cup grated Parmesan cheese
6 ozs. veal kidneys
6 ozs. veal, cut into strips
1 green pepper, cut into strips
1 sweet red pepper, cut into strips
1 onion, chopped
1 clove garlic, peeled and chopped
1 pineapple ring, cut into chunks
⅓ cup water
⅔ cup pineapple juice
2 tablespoons soy sauce
1 tablespoon tomato paste
1 tablespoon vinegar
1 tablespoon honey
salt and pepper
1 chicken bouillon cube
1½ tablespoons cornstarch

1 Boil the spaghetti in a pan of salted water until just tender *(al dente)*. Drain and mix in the butter and 2 tablespoons of the oil. Place in a shallow dish, sprinkle with grated cheese and keep warm.

2 Heat the remaining oil in the skillet. Trim the excess fat and membranes off the kidneys and cut into four. Sauté the kidneys and veal for 4 minutes, then add the peppers, onion and garlic. Cover with a lid and cook for 3 minutes. Add the pineapple, water, pineapple juice, soy sauce, tomato paste, vinegar and honey. Season with the salt and pepper. Crumble in the bouillon cube and boil for 5 minutes. Mix the cornstarch with a little water and stir into the sauce. Boil for 1 minute.

3 Pour the sauce over the spaghetti and serve immediately.

Serves 4

Sweet and Sour Veal Spaghetti is an exciting way of serving kidneys in an oriental sauce

1 The ingredients. Dice onions, carrots, branches of celery and parsley sprigs **2** Put some butter in a casserole, add half the onions and the rest of the vegetables and cook gently without coloring for 2 minutes. Sprinkle with the flour and stir. Cook for 1 minute **3** Add half the red wine and water and stir. Bring to a boil and season with salt, the crushed peppercorns and garlic. Cook for 30 minutes until the vegetables are soft **4** Meanwhile, prepare the kidney by removing the skin from the outside **5** Cut off any fat and the hard white core from the center **6** Cut the kidney into ½-inch slices with a sharp knife **7** Heat some oil in a skillet and brown the kidneys on both sides

quickly **8** Lift out of the pan and keep hot. Discard the cooking juices and fat which should be thrown away **9** Sauté the rest of the chopped onions gently in the butter, in another casserole **10** Add rest of the red wine and boil fast until almost evaporated **11** Add the cooked vegetables and sauce and simmer for 5 minutes **12** Sieve the sauce through a conical strainer gently pressing the softened vegetables through the holes or work through a food mill. Stir to a smooth sauce and check the seasoning and pour over the kidneys and reheat without boiling **13** Place in a serving dish and sprinkle with parsley. Serve hot

Veal Sweetbreads

Sweetbreads are a rich, delicate and highly nutritious food. The best come from the pancreas gland, and only those from calves and lambs are used. They are very rich in protein (22%), contain a good proportion of sodium, and are not, contrary to appearance, fatty. They are a good food for invalids and convalescents because they are easy to digest: the only contra-indication is for people with gout or any excess of uric acid. Their lightness and flavor have made them an important ingredient in classic French cuisine.

Sweetbreads à la Crème

4 calves sweetbreads
pinch salt
juice 2 lemons
2 tablespoons flour, lightly salted
3 tablespoons butter
¼ lb. mushrooms, diced
1 egg yolk
2 tablespoons light cream

1 Soak the sweetbreads in cold, salted water for about 3 hours, changing the water from time to time. Place in a pan, cover with cold water and add a pinch of salt and the juice of 1 lemon. Bring to a boil, then simmer gently for 8 minutes. Cool the sweetbreads under running water and when cold, carefully pick out the gristle and membranes. Dry on absorbent paper.

2 Slice across each sweetbread to make 4 thin slices. Dredge with the flour. Heat the butter in a skillet, add the sweetbreads and sauté lightly until they are golden-brown on each side. Add the mushrooms and sauté for 2 minutes more, then lower the heat, cover, and cook for 15 minutes, until tender. Remove and keep hot.

3 Place the egg yolk and cream in a bowl and beat well together. Pour the juice of the second lemon into the pan and heat through for 2 minutes, scraping the bottom of the pan with a wooden spoon to incorporate the sweetbread and mushroom juices. Take off the heat, stir in the cream mixture, check seasoning and pour over the sweetbreads.

Serves 4

Vol-au-vents Orleans

four puff pastry (vol-au-vent)
  shells, about 4 inches wide
2 sweetbreads
salt
2½ cups water
1 chicken bouillon cube
2 tablespoons wine vinegar
1 onion, sliced
1 carrot, sliced
bouquet garni

For the Sauce:
¼ cup butter
½ cup flour
1¼ cups milk
½ cup dry vermouth
1 cup diced mushrooms

For the Scrambled Eggs:
2 tablespoons butter
2 eggs, beaten
2 tablespoons light cream
pinch paprika

1 Place the prepared pastry shells on a greased baking sheet.

2 Soak the sweetbreads in cold salted water as described in the previous recipe.

3 Bring the water to a boil in a pan. Crumble in the bouillon cube and add the vinegar, onion, carrot and bouquet garni. Season to taste. Add the sweetbreads and simmer for 45 minutes.

4 When the sweetbreads are tender, take them out of the cooking liquor and pick out the gristle and membrane. Cut into small pieces. Strain the liquor and reduce to 1½ cups.

5 Make a roux with 4 tablespoons butter and the flour. Over low heat stir in first the milk, then the reduced stock until the mixture thickens. Check the seasoning. Meanwhile, heat the oven to 350°F. and place the pastry shells cases in the oven to reheat. Heat the vermouth in a pan, add the mushrooms and sweetbreads and simmer gently for 5 minutes. Stir into the sauce.

6 To make the scrambled eggs, heat 2 tablespoons butter in a pan and stir in the eggs and the cream. Season with salt and a pinch of paprika. Take off the heat as soon as they become fluffy and add to the sauce. Take the pastry shells out of the oven, fill with the mixture and serve immediately.

Serves 4

Tip: This mixture can be used to fill small bouchée shells for a buffet party, as shown in the photograph.

Fried Sweetbreads

4 sweetbreads
salt
juice 2 lemons
¼ cup flour
1 teaspoon prepared mustard
1 egg, beaten
½ cup cooked ham, chopped
1½ cups dried breadcrumbs
2 sprigs parsley, chopped
¼ cup butter

1 Soak the sweetbreads in cold, salted water as described in the recipe for Sweetbreads à la Crème. Place them in a pan, cover with cold water and add a pinch of salt and the lemon juice. Bring to a boil and simmer gently for 8 minutes.

2 Cool the sweetbreads under cold running water. Carefully pick out the gristle and membranes. Lay

Vol-au-vents Orleans are filled with sweetbreads in a creamy sauce and make ideal party snacks

them between two plates and place a heavy weight on top to press them for 1-2 hours.

3 Cut the sweetbreads into slices and dredge in the flour. Dilute the mustard with an equal quantity of

water and mix with the beaten egg. Mix together the ham, breadcrumbs and parsley.

4 Coat the sweetbreads with the egg and mustard mixture, then roll in the ham, breadcrumbs and parsley. Heat the butter in a skillet and fry the sweetbreads gently on both sides until they are brown.

Serves 4

Cold Veal

Cold Veal Galantine

one ½-lb. eggplant
1 lb. ground stewing veal
½ lb. ground pork
¼ cup ground bacon
1 onion, chopped
1 cup fresh breadcrumbs
1 tablespoon chopped parsley
salt and pepper
pinch curry powder
pinch garlic salt
1 egg, beaten
6 slices cucumber
3 radishes, sliced

1 Preheat the oven to 400°F.

2 Bake the eggplant in its skin for 15 minutes. Cut in two and scoop out the pulp. Mix in a bowl with the meat, onion, breadcrumbs and parsley, salt and pepper, curry powder and garlic salt. Blend in the beaten egg.

3 Place the meat mixture in a greased, oblong bread pan. Stand the pan in a roasting pan half-filled with water and bake for 1½ hours. Cool and turn out onto a dish. Garnish with the cucumber and radishes.

Serves 6

Veal Roulade

six ¼-lb. veal cutlets
salt and pepper
¼ cup flour
¼ cup oil

For the Stuffing:
5 ozs. diced liver
1 onion, chopped
¼ cup flour
1 egg, beaten
12 asparagus tips, fresh or frozen

For the Chaudfroid Sauce:
1¼ cups white sauce
⅔ cup chicken stock
2 teaspoons unflavored gelatin

1 Beat each cutlet thinly with a mallet or rolling pin on a wet board. Season and dredge with flour.

2 Heat the oil in a skillet and fry the cutlets for 5 minutes on each side. Then cool.

3 Fry the diced liver in the same pan for 4 minutes, add the onion and cook for a further 4 minutes. Stir in the flour and cook for 1 minute.

4 Grind the stuffing mixture finely — twice if necessary — and blend with the beaten egg.

5 Spread this liver stuffing over each cutlet, roll up tightly and wrap in foil. Chill overnight, remove foil and place on a rack.

6 Heat the white sauce. Heat the stock and add the gelatin. Simmer for 2 minutes. Blend half of the gelatin stock with the white sauce and put the remainder aside for glazing and allow to cool.

7 Coat each stuffed veal roll evenly with the chaudfroid sauce. Let cool and set. Then brush with the gelatin. Decorate each roll with two asparagus tips and serve.

Serves 6

Cold Veal Galantine makes a tasty summer lunch; it is also ideal for picnics and buffet parties

Customer service: Box 1000, Brattleboro, VT 05301

Text typesetting in Times Roman and Souvenir
by A & B Typesetters, Inc., Concord NH
Indexes in Helvetica by WordTech Corpor-
ation, Woburn MA
Covers by Federated Lithographers,
Providence RI
Printing and binding by Rand McNally,
Versailles KY
Design and production by Unicorn Produc-
tion Services, Boston MA
Publisher: Tom Begner
Editorial production: Kathy Shulga, Michael
Michaud
Staff: Erika Petersson, Pam Thompson

ISBN 0-914575-03-1

For easy reference, the volumes are numbered
as follows:

1	1-96
2	97-192
3	193-288
4	289-384
5	385-480
6	481-576
7	577-672
8	673-768
9	769-864
10	865-960
11	961-1056
12	1057-1152